THE GIFT

HAFIZ, whose given name was Shams-ud-din Muhammad (c. 1320–1389), is the most beloved poet of Persia. Born in Shiraz, he lived at about the same time as Chaucer in England and about one hundred years after Rumi. He spent nearly all his life in Shiraz, where he became a famous Sufi master. When he died he was thought to have written an estimated 5,000 poems, of which 500 to 700 have survived. His *Divan* (collected poems) is a classic in the literature of Sufism. The work of Hafiz became known to the West largely through the efforts of Goethe, whose enthusiasm rubbed off on Ralph Waldo Emerson, who translated Hafiz in the nineteenth century. Hafiz's poems were also admired by such diverse writers as Nietzsche, Pushkin, Turgenev, Carlyle, and Garcia Lorca; even Sherlock Holmes quotes Hafiz in one of the stories by Arthur Conan Doyle. In 1923, Hazrat Inayat Khan, the Indian teacher often credited with bringing Sufism to the West, proclaimed that "the words of Hafiz have won every heart that listens."

DANIEL LADINSKY was born and raised in St. Louis, Missouri. He has attended several colleges, and has traveled many times around the world. For six years he made his home in a spiritual community in western India, where he worked in a rural clinic free to the poor, and lived with the intimate disciples and family of Meher Baba. Daniel has published two volumes of Hafiz's poetry in translation, *The Subject Tonight Is Love* and *I Heard God Laughing*. He now resides in a small town along the South Carolina coast, where he continues his work with Hafiz.

Also by Daniel Ladinsky

Love Poems from God
Twelve Sacred Voices from the East and West

The Subject Tonight Is Love
60 Wild and Sweet Poems of Hafiz

I Heard God Laughing
Renderings of Hafiz

The Gift

POEMS BY

Hafiz

THE GREAT
SUFI MASTER

Translated by Daniel Ladinsky

PENGUIN COMPASS

PENGUIN COMPASS
Published by the Penguin Group
Penguin Group (USA) Inc., 375 Hudson Street, New York, New York 10014, U.S.A.
Penguin Group (Canada), 90 Eglinton Avenue East, Suite 700, Toronto,
Ontario, Canada M4P 2Y3 (a division of Pearson Penguin Canada Inc.)
Penguin Books Ltd, 80 Strand, London WC2R 0RL, England
Penguin Ireland, 25 St Stephen's Green, Dublin 2, Ireland
(a division of Penguin Books Ltd)
Penguin Group (Australia), 250 Camberwell Road, Camberwell,
Victoria 3124, Australia (a division of Pearson Australia Group Pty Ltd)
Penguin Books India Pvt Ltd, 11 Community Centre, Panchsheel Park,
New Delhi – 110 017, India
Penguin Group (NZ), 67 Apollo Drive, Rosedale, North Shore 0632, New Zealand
(a division of Pearson New Zealand Ltd)
Penguin Books (South Africa) (Pty) Ltd, 24 Sturdee Avenue,
Rosebank, Johannesburg 2196, South Africa

Penguin Books Ltd, Registered Offices: 80 Strand, London WC2R 0RL, England

First published in Compass 1999

36 37 38 39 40

Copyright © Daniel Ladinsky, 1999
All rights reserved

"A Cushion for Your Head," "My Eyes So Soft," and "Only One Rule" first
appeared, under different titles, in *The Subject Tonight Is Love*, versions by Daniel
Ladinsky (Pumpkin House Press, 1996). Copyright © Daniel Ladinsky, 1996.
Grateful acknowledgment is made for permission to reprint "The Life and Work
of Hafiz" by Henry S. Mindlin appearing in *I Heard God Laughing: Renderings of
Hafiz* by Daniel Ladinsky. By permission of Sufism Reoriented, Inc.

LIBRARY OF CONGRESS CATALOGING IN PUBLICATION DATA
Hafiz, 14th cent.
[Divan. English. Selections.]
The gift: poems by Hafiz / the great Sufi master; translated by
Daniel James Ladinsky.
p. cm.
ISBN 978-0-14-019581-1
1. Sufi poetry, Persian—Translations into English. I. Ladinsky,
Daniel James. II. Title.
PK6465.Z31 H34   1999
891'.5511—dc21   99-10920

Printed in the United States of America
Set in Garamond
Designed by Jennifer Ann Daddio

To God's magnificent masquerade—as us!

I am
A hole in a flute
That the Christ's breath moves through—
Listen to this
Music.

—HAFIZ

�֍

ACKNOWLEDGMENTS

A great thanks to a wonderful agent, Thomas Grady; he is a treasure!

A lasting gratitude to friends and family who have enriched this book with their minds and hearts.

Kathleen Barker has helped this work to dance higher. Every poem here has been tuned many times by her love, and with the enchanting music her Tibetan instrument and dulcimer sing.

And thanks to Kathy's dog, Mashuq, who can whirl as well as any dervish. And the way she retrieves a tennis ball batted two hundred feet into the ocean—leaping over waves—makes God a proud Daddy, I'm sure.

Thanks to Sufism Reoriented, in Walnut Creek, California, for permission to reprint Henry S. Mindlin's essay "The Life and Work of Hafiz" from my book *I Heard God Laughing: Renderings of Hafiz.* That essay appears here as the Introduction.

Thanks to Pumpkin House Press, in Myrtle Beach, South Carolina, for permission to use three poems and a few lines of text from my publication *The Subject Tonight Is Love: 60 Wild and Sweet Poems of Hafiz.*

A perennial toast to the many on Hudson Street who believed in this book enough to put their vast talents behind it. A few of those known to me, and who have made significant contributions, are David Stanford, Janet Goldstein, Alexandra Babanskyj, Stephanie Curci, and Leda Scheintaub—you all will be stuck with Christmas cards from me forever.

And I bow to every hand and eye that comes to hold this book and shares Hafiz's extraordinary light with others.

CONTENTS

The Gift

PREFACE

For centuries, Shams-ud-din Muhammad Hafiz (c. 1320–1389) has been a magnificent friend to the human spirit. To millions throughout the world the poems of Hafiz are not a classical work from the remote past, but cherished love, music, wisdom, and humor from a dear companion. These extraordinary verses bestow a precious knowledge. With a wonderful—at times outrageous—genius Hafiz brings us nearer to God. This Persian master is a profound champion of freedom; he constantly encourages our hearts to dance!

Though the West is still getting to know Hafiz, his work has had an intriguing influence here for over two hundred years. One of the earliest translations of a Hafiz poem into English was by Sir William Jones, published in 1771. In the 1800s Ralph Waldo Emerson read Hafiz in German and did several translations of his own into English. In his 1858 "Essay on Persian Poetry," Emerson called Hafiz "a poet for poets" and in his journals wrote: "He fears nothing. He sees too far; he sees throughout; such is the only man I wish to . . . be." Emerson, it is believed, had first found out about

Hafiz in Goethe's 1819 *The West-Eastern Divan.* That work contains a section, called "The Book of Hafiz," in which Goethe enthuses, "In his poetry Hafiz has inscribed undeniable truth indelibly. . . . This is a madness I know well—Hafiz has no peer." In "Open Secret," a poem addressed to Hafiz, Goethe calls him "mystically pure" and at one point calls himself Hafiz's "twin."

Hafiz's poetry is rooted in the beautiful human need for companionship and in the soul's innate desire to surrender all experience—except Light. These verses speak on many levels simultaneously, though they are crafted with such a brilliance rarely does one feel left out.

Hafiz was born and lived in the city of Shiraz. During the preparation of this manuscript I was able to read several of these poems to a Persian friend who comes from generations of Shiraz-born families. She told me, "More copies of the *Divan-i-Hafiz* (the complete collection of his poems) are now sold in Iran than copies of the Quran." This is an amazing fact, given the religious and political climate there. The number of authentic poems that Hafiz left is uncertain and still argued about. That number is presumed to be between five hundred and seven hundred—though this is only 10 percent of his estimated output. The vast majority of his work is said to have been destroyed by clerics and rulers who disapproved of the content of his poems. It is disheartening to contemplate the loss of so much beauty and divine intelligence from this world. Hafiz was viewed as a great threat, a spiritual rebel, whose insights emancipate his readers from the clutches of those in power—those who exploit the innocent with insane religious propaganda. For Hafiz reveals a God with a billion I.Q.—a God that would never cripple us with guilt or control us with fear.

One of the reasons for Hafiz's great popularity is that for centuries he has been considered a living oracle able to impart the most intimate, timely advice. The typical reader of Hafiz's poems turns to them as one might turn to an astrologer, a horoscope, or a medium. It is said that Queen Victoria used to consult Hafiz in this manner.

Hafiz's message is as relevant now as it was when he wrote in the fourteenth century. He continues to offer all seekers a spiritual recovery and intricate help with the heart's imperative—its destined, glorious unfolding of love. "My spring eyes will still warm faces, and awake verdant earths in your soul."

People from many religious traditions share the belief that there are always living persons who are one with God. These rare souls disseminate light upon this earth and entrust the Divine to others. Hafiz is regarded as one who came to live in that sacred union, and sometimes in his poems he speaks directly of that experience.

Someone once wrote to me, responding to my first two Hafiz publications, "How could anyone ever say they were God?" I answered, "If God exists, if a Real God exists—one of Infinite Power—then there is Nothing that God could not do. That is, the physics become simple: If God wanted, He could give Himself entirely to someone without ever diminishing His own state. And if you were the recipient of that Divine Gift—what would you then know?"

Rumi, Kabir, Saadi, Shams, Francis of Assisi, Ramakrishna, Nanak, Milarepa, and Lao-tzu are among the many known to have achieved perfection or Union because of their extraordinary romance with the Beloved. They are sometimes called "realized souls" or "Perfect Masters." As Hafiz wrote:

The voice of the river that has emptied into the Ocean
Now laughs and sings just like God.

I believe that the adoption of sanctified poetry from one culture to another, such as we are now witnessing on a large scale, heralds the next conscious step of evolution of the adopting language. True art evolves us—opens our arms and weakens our prejudices so that the ever-present seeds of healing and renewal can take root in our soul and sinew, cause joy.

I began working with these poems by translating from Farsi (Persian) into English, which was remarkably demanding. I was aided by an unexpected gift; a friend in India sent me a complete photocopy of the most respected English translation of Hafiz, that of H. Wilberforce Clarke. Clarke's work was first published in India in 1891. This was a copy of the rare 1971 Samuel Weiser edition—only five hundred were ever printed. All of the poems in this book are based on Clarke's translations and his vast footnotes. I also draw on several thousand pages of other material about Hafiz's life, and on other poems attributed to Hafiz. It is a tremendous venture to translate an "untranslatable" masterpiece such as Hafiz's verse, with its brilliant whirling synergy of idioms, especially into a language as spiritually young and evolving as English. I believe the ultimate gauge of success is this: Does the text free the reader? Does it contribute to our physical and emotional health? Does it put "golden tools" into our hands that can help excavate the Beloved whom we and society have buried so deep inside?

Persian poets of Hafiz's era would often address themselves in their poems, making the poem an intimate conversation. This was also a method of "signing" the poem, as one might sign a letter to a friend, or a painting. It should also be noted that sometimes Hafiz speaks as a seeker, other times as a master and guide.

Hafiz also has a unique vocabulary of names for God—as one might have endearing pet names for one's own family members. To Hafiz, God is more than just the Father, the Mother, the Infinite, or a Being beyond comprehension. Hafiz gives God a vast range of names, such as Sweet Uncle, the Generous Merchant, the Problem Giver, the Problem Solver, the Friend, the Beloved. The words *Ocean, Sky, Sun, Moon,* and *Love,* among others, when capitalized in these poems, can sometimes be synonyms for God, as it is a Hafiz trait to offer these poems to many levels of interpretation simultaneously. To Hafiz, God is Someone we can meet, enter, and eternally explore.

My editor felt that a few words needed to be said about the general architecture of this book, specifically, *why so many chapters?* Well, would it make sense if I said that I felt Hafiz didn't want anything to get sore. That is, some honeymooners could benefit with a room-service waiter knocking now and then, or a phone call from

Mom, causing a pause in the action, an intermission, a moment to contemplate and digest.

I might also mention here that once in a while I may seem to have taken the liberty to play a few of these lines through a late-night jazz sax instead of from a morning temple drum or lyre. To some readers a few expressions in this book may appear too contemporary for this work. To that I say—nothing doing. The word *translation* comes from the Latin for "to bring across." My goal is to *bring across,* right into your lap, the wondrous spirit of Hafiz that lifts the corners of the mouth. I view this goal as a primary, no-holds-barred task. And I apologize for any language that may stop the beguine and not let the reader remain in Hafiz's tender strong embrace.

An interesting trait of Hafiz that should be noted is that he occasionally "sells" himself, as it were. I have come to feel that this is his response to the spiritual marketplace's sometimes becoming filled with sham teachers who lace their bread with harmful additives. He knows that a lot of what is sold with God's name on it isn't *organic.* Thus Hafiz may be trying to safeguard us, draw us near, when he says things like, "My words nourish even the sun's body. Look at the smile on the earth's lips this morning, she laid with me again last night." "The sublime amorous ghazals of Hafiz," García Lorca once said.

I have been intensely involved with these poems for several years; for the last three years I have averaged some sixty hours per week with some facet of them. My work with Hafiz began in the fall of 1992, on an early morning walk in the countryside of western India, on a beautiful tree-lined road that leads to the former residence of Meher Baba, who passed away in 1969. I was walking with an elderly Zoroastrian man, someone whom I have known for twenty years, have lived close to and consider a teacher, a brother, a cherished friend. I would say that it is because of this man's and his master's (Meher Baba) profound respect for Hafiz that this book now appears. I feel my relationship with Hafiz defies reason and is really an attempt to do the impossible: to translate Light into words—to make the luminous resonance of God tangible to our finite senses. About six months into this work I had an astounding dream in which I saw Hafiz as an Infinite Fountaining Sun (I saw him as God), who sang hundreds of lines of his poetry to me in English, asking me to give that message to his "artists and seekers."

Every line of Hafiz that I have wept over—and there have been many—increased my desire to impart his remarkable qualities: an audacious encouragement, his outrageous onslaught of love, a transforming knowledge and generosity, his sweet-playful exuberant genius that is unparalleled in world literature. There is a mystical dimension in his poetry that heals and bestows "The Gift." There is dulcet language that rises from his reed-soul, the voice of one "startled by God." His words are a *music* that comforts, empowers, enlightens.

Hafiz is one of the greatest spiritual friends, lovers, and guides that humankind has ever known. For centuries he has been called the Tongue of the Invisible, for he continues to sing beautiful and wild love songs from God. He invites us to join him in his fantastic applause of life. I vote to inscribe these words of Hafiz on every flag, church bell, temple, mosque, and politician's brain:

Dear ones, let's anoint this earth with dance!

Daniel Ladinsky
January 31, 1999

❀

INTRODUCTION:

The Life and Work of Hafiz

Despite the popularity of Hafiz in the East, reliable information about the details of his life is sketchy. Scholars do not even agree about his dates of birth and death. He was probably born about 1320 and died about 1389, roughly the same dates as the first great poet who wrote in English, Geoffrey Chaucer. His given name was Shams-ud-din Muhammad. He chose the name Hafiz ("memorizer") as a pen name when he began to write poetry; it is a title given to someone who knows the entire Quran by heart, as he apparently did. Hafiz was born in Shiraz, a beautiful city in southern Persia that escaped the ravages of the Mongol and Tartar invasions during this violent and chaotic period of history. He spent nearly all of his life in this cultured garden city.

EARLY LIFE

All is written within the mind
To help and instruct the dervish
In dance and romance and prayer.

7

Hafiz did not have an easy or comfortable life. He was the youngest of three sons of poor parents. His father was a coal merchant who died when Hafiz was in his teens. To help support the family, Hafiz worked as a baker's assistant by day and put himself through school at night, using part of his salary to pay his tuition. Over many years, he mastered the subjects of a "classical" medieval education: Quranic law and theology, grammar, mathematics, and astronomy. He also mastered calligraphy, which in the centuries before printing was a highly refined art form. Islamic calligraphy was originally developed as a sacred art to preserve and glorify the Quran, the message of God. Since representational art was forbidden by religious law, calligraphy reached a remarkable degree of subtlety and expressiveness. Hafiz was a skilled draftsman and occasionally worked as a professional copyist.

His early education naturally included the great Persian poets: Saadi of Shiraz, Farid-ud-din Attar, Jalal-ud-din Rumi, and others. Poetry is a national art in Persia, somewhat like opera in Italy. Even in modern Iran, people at every social level know the great poets, argue passionately about their favorites, and quote them constantly in everyday conversation. In medieval Persia, the art of poetry was taken seriously and valued highly. Local princes and provincial governors employed court poets to create epic verses celebrating their greatness. When the ruler was especially pleased by a composition, the poet was sometimes placed on a scale and rewarded with his weight in gold.

A POET

A poet is someone
Who can pour light into a cup,
Then raise it to nourish
Your beautiful parched, holy mouth.

Hafiz had a natural poetic gift. Even as a child, he was able to im-
provise poems on any subject in any form and style. When he was
in his early twenties, some of his love poems began to circulate in
Shiraz, and he was soon invited to participate in poetry gatherings
at court. He won the patronage of a succession of rulers and wealthy
noblemen. One of his benefactors founded a religious college and
offered Hafiz a position as a teacher. Thus, during his middle years,
he served as a court poet and a college professor. He married and
had at least one son.

Hafiz's livelihood depended solely on patronage. Everyone ad-
mired his literary brilliance, but his poetry boldly celebrated ideas
that bordered on heresy, and he had enemies among the rigorously
orthodox who "blacklisted" him whenever they came to power. Pe-
riodically, he would fall out of favor and lose his position, both at
court and in the college. He would sometimes use his skills as a
copyist to support his family until his fortunes improved. At least
once, however, he was forced to leave Shiraz. For several years he
lived as an exile, often in dire poverty. Finally a new, more tolerant
regime allowed him to return home and resume his career. During
the long, unsettled middle period of his life, first his son and later
his wife passed away. Some scholars associate many of his deeply felt
verses of grief, separation, and loss with these events.

By the time he was sixty, Hafiz had become famous as a master
poet. A circle of students and companions gathered around him,
and he served them as a teacher and counselor until his quiet death
at about the age of seventy. He was buried in one of his favorite
spots, at the foot of a cypress tree he himself had planted in a rose
garden near Shiraz. For five hundred years his tomb, surrounded by
the rose garden, was a center of pilgrimage and refreshment for
thousands. By the early twentieth century, however, the tomb had
fallen into disrepair. Then, in 1925, arrangements were made with
the Persian government to have a new structure built over the grave
and to have the gardens gradually restored. These arrangements
were initiated and partially funded by a contemporary spiritual fig-

ure from India who loved Hafiz, Avatar Meher Baba. This modern world teacher frequently quoted couplets of Hafiz to illustrate his own discussions of spiritual principles. Meher Baba explained that the love poetry of Hafiz contained all the secrets of the spiritual path—for the true subject matter of spirituality is Love.

SPIRITUAL STUDENT

We have been in love with God
For so very, very long.

Hafiz was, in fact, a spiritual student. As a young man, he became a disciple of a Sufi teacher who guided him through a difficult spiritual apprenticeship that lasted most of his adult life. Later, Hafiz himself became a Sufi master. His *Divan* (collected poems) is a classic in the literature of Sufism, an ancient spiritual tradition whose special emphasis is intense, often ecstatic, one-pointed devotion to God.

In the West, Sufism is usually regarded as a form of Islamic mysticism. However, the Sufis themselves say their "way" has always existed, under many names, in many lands, associated with the mystical dimension of every spiritual system. In ancient Greece, for example, they were identified with the wisdom (*sophia*) schools of Pythagoras and Plato. At the time of Jesus, they were called Essenes or Gnostics. After Muhammad, they adopted many of the principles and formulations of Islam and became known in the Muslim world as "Sufis," a word given various meanings, including "wisdom," "purity," and "wool" (for the coarse woolen habits of wandering dervishes).

From about 800 to 1400 A.D., Sufi schools flourished under the guidance of master teachers such as Rumi and Ibn Arabi. As individual schools developed, their methods of teaching diversified according to the needs of each group. Some stressed formal meditation, others focused on selfless service to the world, and still others emphasized devotional practices: song, dance, and spiritual poetry celebrating love for God. The Sufis cherish the poetry of Hafiz as a perfect expression of the human experience of divine love.

How Hafiz came to be a Sufi student is a famous and popular story told in many versions throughout the East:

It is said that when he was twenty-one and working as a baker's assistant, Hafiz delivered some bread to a mansion and happened to catch a fleeting glimpse of a beautiful girl on the terrace. That one glimpse captured his heart, and he fell madly in love with her, though she did not even notice him. She was from a wealthy noble family, and he was a poor baker's assistant. She was beautiful, he was short and physically unattractive—the situation was hopeless.

As months went by, Hafiz made up poems and love songs celebrating her beauty and his longing for her. People heard him singing his poems and began to repeat them; the poems were so touching that they became popular all over Shiraz.

Hafiz was oblivious of his new fame as a poet; he thought only of his beloved. Desperate to win her, he undertook an arduous spiritual discipline that required him to keep a vigil at the tomb of a certain saint all night long for forty nights. It was said that anyone who could accomplish this near-impossible austerity would be granted his heart's desire. Every day Hafiz went to work at the bakery. Every night he went to the saint's tomb and willed himself to stay awake for love of this girl. His love was so strong that he succeeded in completing this vigil.

At daybreak on the fortieth day, the archangel Gabriel appeared before Hafiz and told him to ask for whatever he wished. Hafiz had never seen such a glorious, radiant being as Gabriel. He found himself thinking, "If God's messenger is so beautiful, how much more beautiful must God be!" Gazing on the unimaginable splendor of God's angel, Hafiz forgot all about the girl, his wish, everything. He said, "I want God!"

Gabriel then directed Hafiz to a spiritual teacher who lived in

Shiraz. The angel told Hafiz to serve this teacher in every way and his wish would be fulfilled. Hafiz hurried to meet his teacher, and they began their work together that very day.

HAFIZ AND HIS TEACHER

Our Partner is notoriously difficult to follow,
And even His best musicians are not always easy
To hear.

The teacher's name was Muhammad Attar. *Attar* signifies a chemist or perfumer, and it is believed that Muhammad Attar owned a shop in Shiraz and lived a very ordinary public life. Only his small circle of students knew him as a spiritual teacher.

Hafiz visited Attar nearly every day for years. They sat together, sometimes dined together, sometimes talked, sometimes sang, sometimes went for quiet walks in the beautiful rose gardens of Shiraz. Attar opened Hafiz's vision to fresh, ever deeper perceptions of the beauty and harmony of life and a much broader understanding of all the processes of love. It was natural for Hafiz to express these insights in the language of poetry. Muhammad Attar was also a poet, and he encouraged Hafiz in this direction. For many years, Hafiz created a poem a day for his teacher. Attar told his students to collect and study these poems, for they illustrated many of the central principles of spiritual unfolding.

However, the relationship between Hafiz and his teacher was not always an easy one. In many accounts, Muhammad Attar is presented as a stern and demanding figure who sometimes appeared to show no compassion at all for Hafiz. Modern spiritual figures, notably Avatar Meher Baba, have used the example of Hafiz and Attar to illustrate how challenging and difficult it can be to serve an authentic spiritual teacher. In his discourses on the role of the master, Meher Baba explains that, regardless of external appearances, a teacher must always aid internal processes of growth that support increasingly broader designs of love. Along the way, the student's limited ego is dissolved—or, as Hafiz says, ground to dust. Meher Baba described this process as "hell on earth" for Hafiz. He said, "Hafiz, so to speak, broke his head at the feet of his master," day after day, year after year, for forty long years.

Some stories about Hafiz and his teacher support this view. Often Hafiz is portrayed as running to Attar in despair, pleading for enlightenment or spiritual liberation after decades of frustration. Each time, Attar would tell Hafiz to be patient and wait, and all would be revealed. According to one account:

One day, when Hafiz was well over sixty, he confronted his aged teacher and said, "Look at me! I'm old, my wife and son are long dead. What have I gained by being your obedient disciple for all these years?" Attar gently replied, "Be patient and one day you will know." Hafiz shouted, "I knew I would get that answer from you!" In a fever of spiritual desperation, he began another form of forty-day vigil. This time he drew a circle on the ground and sat within it for forty days and nights, without leaving it for food, drink, or even to relieve himself. On the fortieth day, the angel again appeared to him and asked what he desired. Hafiz discovered that during the forty days all his desires had disappeared. He replied instantly that his only wish was to serve his teacher.

Just before dawn Hafiz came out of the circle and went to his teacher's house. Attar was waiting at the door. They embraced warmly, and Attar gave Hafiz a special cup of aged wine. As they drank together, the intoxicating joy of the wine opened his heart and dissolved every trace of separateness. With a great laugh of delight, Hafiz was forever drowned in love and united with God, his divine Beloved.

It is said that Hafiz unknowingly began his vigil *exactly* forty days before the end of his fortieth year of service to his teacher and that the "moment of union" was exactly forty years to the day from the moment they first met.

LEVELS OF LOVE

All I know is Love,
And I find my heart Infinite
And Everywhere!

Many of these vignettes about Hafiz have the charming symmetry and precision of symbolic teaching stories. The recurring number forty, for example, might not be meant literally. In spiritual literature, "forty" is often used to indicate a term of learning or change, such as the "forty days and forty nights" of Noah's Flood. Forty is also called "the number of perseverance," marking a period of growth through testing, trial, and purification. After the exodus from Egypt, the Israelites endured "forty years of wandering" in the wilderness before they were ready to enter the Promised Land. Jesus, following the ancient practice of the prophets, went into the desert for a great seclusion of forty days, which he described as a period of purification and preparation for the next stage of his work. The Buddha attained final enlightenment after forty days of continuous meditation. One can find many examples, East and West.

These tales of Hafiz share other common symbols. There is the "mystic circle," which is an image of completion or perfection. And there is the glass of wine Attar gives Hafiz. A glass or cup is a vessel, which can often represent the human heart, or even the human being as a vessel of love. "Wine" stands for love in many spiritual traditions. Aged wine, such as Attar shares with Hafiz, can represent the purified (distilled) essence of knowing or love.

As teaching stories, these episodes can be seen to illustrate central stages of the Sufi "path of love" or inner unfolding:

Hafiz begins his spiritual journey as nearly everyone does—he is awakened to love. An ideal of human beauty and perfection seizes his heart. Desperate to win his ideal, he fully explores the realm of human love (his poems and songs celebrate her beauty and his longing for her).

Finally, he directs all the energies of his life to the pursuit of love (a forty-day vigil).

When his longing reaches its highest pitch (dawn of the final day), *a new and higher dimension of love reveals itself* (Gabriel). *He is able to respond to the beauty of this higher understanding* ("I want God!"), *and his response ushers him into a new phase of learning and a new relationship of love* (with a spiritual teacher).

This new term of growth (forty years) *is exponentially longer than the first one. Attar leads Hafiz through a review of increasingly broader and more encompassing levels of love* (a poem a day). *Hafiz becomes restless as his love for God grows stronger. Attar constantly counsels "patience" to remind Hafiz that every stage of love must be fully explored, honored, and lived.*

As the term nears its end, Hafiz reaches a new height of desperation and longing for his Beloved. He again seeks to devote all his energies to love (another forty-day vigil). *This time he binds himself within a circle* (of perfection or completion), *literally circumscribing all his thoughts and actions to a single focus—God. He strives to perfect his love for God until nothing else exists for him.*

When he has truly accomplished this (dawn of the final day), *he finds that the force of love has consumed his limited personality and all its desires, even the desire for God. He has realized that one cannot "master" love, one can only serve as a vessel of love* (a glass of wine).

Emerging from the circle, Hafiz is now able to approach and embrace every experience of life with the unlimited wisdom of love (he and his teacher embrace). *He and Attar now share the same perfect knowing* (the aged wine of love's maturity). *The "glass of aged wine" now becomes a symbol for "the embodiment of perfect love"—Hafiz himself.*

PERFECTION

I hear the voice
Of every creature and plant,
Every world and sun and galaxy—
Singing the Beloved's Name!

The idea that a human being can achieve "perfect love" or "perfect knowing" may seem extraordinary, yet it is a belief shared by most spiritual systems. It is called by many names—union with the Father, *nirvikalpa samadhi,* the highest development of consciousness, God-realization, *Qutubiyat,* or simply Perfection. One who attains it can be called a Perfect Master, someone who embodies a perfect understanding of the beauty and harmony of the universe.

A Perfect Master experiences life as an infinite and continuous flow of divine love, swirling in, around and through all forms of life and all realms of creation. It is an experience of total unity with all life and all beings. A Perfect Master personifies perfect joy, perfect knowing, and perfect love and expresses these qualities in every activity of life.

In the Western world, the most familiar example of such perfect love may be Francis of Assisi. In the East, there have been many— Rumi in Persia, Kabir and Ramakrishna in India, Milarepa in Tibet, Lao-tzu in China are all revered as Perfect Masters.*

The teacher of Hafiz, Muhammad Attar, was a Perfect Master, and so was Hafiz himself. The poetry of Hafiz can be read as a

---

*World Teachers such as Jesus, Buddha, Krishna, and Muhammad also exemplify perfection—Personified.

record of a human being's journey to perfect joy, perfect knowing, and perfect love.

MASTER POET

Write a thousand luminous secrets
Upon the wall of existence
So that even a blind man will know
Where we are,
And join us in this love!

Hafiz developed his poetry under the guidance of his teacher. Muhammad Attar reviewed and discussed the poems in his teaching circle, and many of them were set to music. This was a common practice in Sufi schools of the time, including Rumi's order of "whirling dervishes" in Turkey. Poetry and song, easy to memorize and repeat, were used as teaching materials to encapsulate or summarize spiritual principles. With Attar's encouragement, Hafiz perfected this teaching method using a popular form of love song, the *ghazal*. He wrote hundreds of *ghazals*, finding ways to bring new depth and meaning to the lyrics without losing the accustomed association of a love song.

His poems expressed every nuance and stage of his growing understanding of love. He wrote of the game of love, the beauty of the Beloved, the sweet pain of longing, the agony of waiting, the ecstatic joy of union. He explored different forms and levels of love: his delight in nature's beauty, his romantic courtship of that ideal unattainable girl, his sweet affection for his wife, his tender feelings for his child—and his terrible grief and loneliness when, later in his life, both his wife and his son passed away. He wrote of his relationship with his teacher and his adoration of God.

All who heard his poetry could easily associate it with their own most cherished experiences of love. The familiar rhythms of the love song, the *ghazal,* made the poems easy to learn. Before long, his poems were sung all over Persia by people from every walk of life—farmers, craftsmen, scholars, princes, even children.

Many who knew of Hafiz and enjoyed his poetry had no idea that he was a Sufi. Nor did many people know the spiritual status of his teacher. Like many Sufi masters of his time, Muhammad Attar met with his students in secret, and Hafiz did not reveal his own association with Attar until after his master's death. In the religious climate of medieval Persia, this secrecy was essential. From time to time, waves of what might be called fanatical fundamentalism swept through the country. To these fundamentalists, it was blasphemy to suggest that any human being could attain perfection or approach direct knowledge of divinity. The Sufi schools were frequently outlawed, and many of their adherents were tried and executed. Those who survived were forced to meet in secret and disguise their teachings in a symbolic language that would not offend the orthodox. This became the language of Sufi poetry. Images of wine and the Tavern came to represent love and the Sufi school; the nightingale and the Rose were the lover and the Beloved. Spiritual students were depicted as clowns, beggars, scoundrels, rogues, courtesans, or intoxicated wayfarers.

This symbolic language developed gradually over hundreds of years. Hafiz brought it to perfection in his poetry. Even today, people argue about the "true" meaning of his verses—is he simply describing the joy of walking in the garden or speaking symbolically about God's delight in the material forms of His Creation? Or both? When he praises a wealthy patron or the charms of a young woman, is he really celebrating God, his true Patron and Beloved? Perhaps both. For Hafiz does not see God as separate from the world—wherever there is love, there is the Beloved. The Indian Sufi teacher Inayat Khan explained, "The mission of Hafiz was to express to a fanatical religious world that the presence of God is not to be found only in heaven, but also here on earth."

In Persian, Hafiz is sometimes called the Tongue of the Invisible, for so many of his poems seem to be ecstatic and beautiful love songs from God to His beloved world. Hafiz shares his intoxication with the magic and beauty of divine life that pulsates everywhere around us and within us. He urges us to rise on the wings of love. He challenges us to confront and master the strongest forces of our own nature. He encourages us to celebrate even the most ordinary experiences of life as precious divine gifts. He invites us to "awake awhile" and listen to the delightful music of God's laughter.

> What is this precious love and laughter
> Budding in our hearts?
> It is the glorious sound
> Of a soul waking up!

ONE

Startled by God

Not like

A lone beautiful bird

These poems now rise in great white flocks

Against my mind's vast hills

Startled by God

Breaking a branch

When His foot

Touches

Earth

Near

Me.

LET'S EAT

Why

Just show you God's menu?

Hell, we are all

Starving—

Let's

Eat!

WHEN THE VIOLIN

When
The violin
Can forgive the past

It starts singing.

When the violin can stop worrying
About the future

You will become
Such a drunk laughing nuisance

That God
Will then lean down
And start combing you into
His
Hair.

When the violin can forgive
Every wound caused by
Others

The heart starts
Singing.

LOOKING FOR GOOD FISH

Why complain about life
If you are looking for good fish
And have followed some idiot
Into the middle of the copper market?

Why go crazy
If you are looking for fine silk
And you keep rubbing your hands against
Burlap and hemp sacks?

If your heart really needs to touch a face
That is filled with abundance
Then why didn't you come to this
Old Man sooner?

For my cheek is the universe's cloister
And if you can make your prayers sweet enough
Tonight

Then Hafiz will lean over and offer you
All the warmth in my body
In case God is busy
Doing something else
Somewhere.

Why complain if you are looking
To quench your spirit's longing
And have followed a rat into a desert.

If your soul really needs to touch a face
That is always filled with compassion

And tenderness
Then why,

Why my dear
Did you not come to your friend Hafiz
Sooner?

A HUNTING PARTY

A

Hunting party

Sometimes has a greater chance

Of flushing love and God

Out into the open

Than a warrior

All

Alone.

THIS SANE IDEA

Let your
Intelligence begin to rule
Whenever you sit with others

Using this sane idea:

Leave all your cocked guns in a field
Far from us,

One of those damn things
Might go

Off.

WE HAVE NOT COME TO
TAKE PRISONERS

We have not come here to take prisoners,
But to surrender ever more deeply
To freedom and joy.

We have not come into this exquisite world
To hold ourselves hostage from love.

Run my dear,
From anything
That may not strengthen
Your precious budding wings.

Run like hell my dear,
From anyone likely
To put a sharp knife
Into the sacred, tender vision
Of your beautiful heart.

We have a duty to befriend
Those aspects of obedience
That stand outside of our house
And shout to our reason
"O please, O please,
Come out and play."

For we have not come here to take prisoners
Or to confine our wondrous spirits,

But to experience ever and ever more deeply
Our divine courage, freedom, and
Light!

I CAN SEE ANGELS

I can
See angels
Sitting on your ears,

Polishing trumpets,
Replacing lute strings,
Stretching new skins on the drums
And gathering wood for the evening's fire.

They all danced last night
But you did not
Hear them.

If you ask Hafiz for advice
On how to befriend their sweet voices
And how to have the nourishing
Company of the finer
Worlds

I would reply,

"I could not say anything
You could not
Tell me."

Then,
What was the use of this story?

O,
I just felt like
Talking.

YOU'RE IT

God
Disguised
As a myriad things and
Playing a game
Of tag

Has kissed you and said,
"You're it—

I mean, you're Really IT!"

Now
It does not matter
What you believe or feel

For something wonderful,

Major-league Wonderful
Is someday going
To

Happen.

I RAIN

I rain
Because your meadows call
For God.

I weave light into words so that
When your mind holds them

Your eyes will relinquish their sadness,
Turn bright, a little brighter, giving to us
The way a candle does
To the dark.

I have wrapped my laughter like a birthday gift
And left it beside your bed.

I have planted the wisdom in my heart
Next to every signpost in the sky.

A wealthy man
Often becomes eccentric,

A divine crazed soul
Is transformed into infinite generosity

Tying gold sacks of gratuity
To the dangling feet of moons, planets, ecstatic
Midair dervishes, and singing birds.

I speak
Because every cell in your body
Is reaching out
For God.

I Have Learned So Much

I
Have
Learned
So much from God
That I can no longer
Call
Myself

A Christian, a Hindu, a Muslim,
A Buddhist, a Jew.

The Truth has shared so much of Itself
With me

That I can no longer call myself
A man, a woman, an angel,
Or even pure
Soul.

Love has
Befriended Hafiz so completely
It has turned to ash
And freed
Me

Of every concept and image
My mind has ever known.

GOD JUST CAME NEAR

No

One

In need of love

Can sit with my verse for

An hour

And then walk away without carrying

Golden tools,

And feeling that God

Just came

Near.

THE SUN NEVER SAYS

Even
After
All this time
The sun never says to the earth,

"You owe
Me."

Look
What happens
With a love like that,
It lights the
Whole
Sky.

THE SEED CRACKED OPEN

It used to be
That when I would wake in the morning
I could with confidence say,
"What am 'I' going to
Do?"

That was before the seed
Cracked open.

Now Hafiz is certain:

There are two of us housed
In this body,

Doing the shopping together in the market and
Tickling each other
While fixing the evening's food.

Now when I awake
All the internal instruments play the same music:

"God, what love-mischief can 'We' do
For the world
Today?"

WHY JUST ASK THE DONKEY

Why
Just ask the donkey in me
To speak to the donkey in you,

When I have so many other beautiful animals
And brilliant colored birds inside
That are all longing to say something wonderful
And exciting to your heart?

Let's open all the locked doors upon our eyes
That keep us from knowing the Intelligence
That begets love
And a more lively and satisfying conversation
With the Friend.

Let's turn loose our golden falcons
So that they can meet in the sky
Where our spirits belong—
Necking like two
Hot kids.

Let's hold hands and get drunk near the sun
And sing sweet songs to God
Until He joins us with a few notes
From His own sublime lute and drum.

If you have a better idea
Of how to pass a lonely night
After your glands may have performed
All their little magic

Then speak up sweethearts, speak up,
For Hafiz and all the world will listen.

Why just bring your donkey to me
Asking for stale hay
And a boring conference with the idiot
In regards to this precious matter—
Such a precious matter as love,

When I have so many other divine animals
And brilliant colored birds inside
That are all longing
To so sweetly
Greet
You!

WHO WROTE ALL THE MUSIC

Why is it now
That I come to you like a humble servant
Willing to feed you brilliant words and love
From my own sacred mouth and hands,

Willing to say, "I am sorry,
I am sorry for all your pain"?

It is because when God
Fully revealed Himself in me

I saw that it was Hafiz
Who wrote all the music you have been playing.

I saw it was Hafiz
Who wrote all your notes of sadness,
But also etched and gave you
Every ecstatic wince of joy your face, body,
And heart has ever known.

Okay my dear,
You have stumbled enough in the earth's sweet dance.
You have paid all your dues
Many times.

Now let's get down to the real reason
Why we sit together and breathe

And begin the laughing, the divine laughing,
Like great heroic women
And magnificent
Strong men.

YOUR MOTHER AND MY MOTHER

Fear is the cheapest room in the house.
I would like to see you living
In better conditions,

For your mother and my mother
Were friends.

I know the Innkeeper
In this part of the universe.
Get some rest tonight,
Come to my verse again tomorrow.
We'll go speak to the Friend together.

I should not make any promises right now,
But I know if you
Pray
Somewhere in this world—
Something good will happen.

God wants to see
More love and playfulness in your eyes
For that is your greatest witness to Him.

Your soul and my soul
Once sat together in the Beloved's womb
Playing footsie.

Your heart and my heart
Are very, very old
Friends.

MISMATCHED NEWLYWEDS

Like

A pair

Of mismatched newlyweds,

One of whom still feels very insecure,

I keep turning to God

Saying,

"Kiss

Me."

YOUR SEED POUCH

Lanterns
Hang from the night sky
So that your eye might draw
One more image of love upon your silk canvas
Before sleep.

Words from Him have reached you
And tilled a golden field inside.

When all your desires are distilled
You will cast just two votes:

To love more,
And be happy.

Take the sounds from the mouth-flute of Hafiz
And mix them into your seed pouch.

And when the Moon says,
"It is time to
Plant,"

Why not dance,
Dance and
Sing?

THAT MAGNIFICENT STORM

Sitting here
Loving like this

Alone again
In God's valley
After that magnificent storm
Of Your presence just
Passed,

I am like an elegant cypress
Whose face and form
Your beauty
Ruined.

Why not
Accuse You of infidelity
Or much
Worse

When every
Lover of God in this world
Would gladly
Testify

On
My
Behalf.

Removing the Shoe from the Temple

Once someone asked me,

"Why do saints seek divine annihilation
And are often humble
And like to spend their free time
Upon their knees?"

I replied,

"It is a simple matter of etiquette."

Then they said,

"What do you mean, Hafiz?"

"Well," I continued,
"When ones goes into a mosque or temple
Is it not common to remove what
Covers your
Feet?

So too does it happen
With this whole mind and body—
That is something like a shoe sole—

When one begins to realize
Upon Whom you are really standing,

One begins
To remove the 'shoe' from the
Temple."

AGAINST MY OWN HAND

You are
A shy divine deer
That I cannot cease tracking.

Though only once of late
Did I get so close
To see

My own face and heart
Reflected

In Your wondrous soft eyes.

Only once of late, Beloved,
When I thought that I had You
At last cornered

Did
Hafiz
Come to know
The sublime beauty of God's body

Against my own
Hand.

OUT OF THIS MESS

Pray
To be humble
So that God does not
Have to appear to be so stingy.

O pray to be honest,
Strong,
Kind,
And pure,

So that the Beloved is never miscast
As a cruel great miser.

I know you have a hundred complex cases
Against God in court,

But never mind, wayfarer,
Let's just get out of this mess

And pray to be loving and humble
So that the Friend will be forced to reveal

Himself
So

Near!

IF GOD INVITED YOU
TO A PARTY

If God
Invited you to a party
And said,

"Everyone
In the ballroom tonight
Will be my special
Guest,"

How would you then treat them
When you
Arrived?

Indeed, indeed!

And Hafiz knows
There is no one in this world

Who
Is not upon
His Jeweled Dance
Floor.

TO BUILD A SWING

You carry
All the ingredients
To turn your life into a nightmare—
Don't mix them!

You have all the genius
To build a swing in your backyard
For God.

That sounds
Like a hell of a lot more fun.
Let's start laughing, drawing blueprints,
Gathering our talented friends.

I will help you
With my divine lyre and drum.

Hafiz
Will sing a thousand words
You can take into your hands,
Like golden saws,
Silver hammers,

Polished teakwood,
Strong silk rope.

You carry all the ingredients
To turn your existence into joy,

Mix them, mix
Them!

A CRYSTAL RIM

The
Earth
Lifts its glass to the sun
And light—light
Is poured.

A bird
Comes and sits on a crystal rim
And from my forest cave I
Hear singing,

So I run to the edge of existence
And join my soul in love.

I lift my heart to God
And grace is poured.

An emerald bird rises from inside me
And now sits
Upon the Beloved's
Glass.

I have left that dark cave forever.
My body has blended with His.

I lay my wing
As a bridge to you

So that you can join us
Singing.

THIS ONE IS MINE

Someone put
You on a slave block
And the unreal bought
You.

Now I keep coming to your owner
Saying,

"This one is mine."

You often overhear us talking
And this can make your heart leap
With excitement.

Don't worry,
I will not let sadness
Possess you.

I will gladly borrow all the gold
I need

To get you
Back.

CURFEWS

Noise
Is a cruel ruler

Who is always imposing
Curfews,

While
Stillness and quiet
Break open the vintage
Bottles,

Awake the real
Band.

THE EAR THAT WAS SOLD
TO A FISH

It is true.
I once had an ear that got sold to a fish.
Lean back: I will be glad to tell you all about
How it happened,
But first I must digress a bit,
Perhaps way beyond any logical sequence
Of events
We may ever again piece together.

Let's see,
We could start anywhere,
With any word,
In this fertile luminous world in which I live.

What is the first letter of your alphabet?

A,
O—
That will be just fine.

Art is the conversation between lovers.
Art offers an opening for the heart.
True art makes the divine silence in the soul
Break into applause.

Art is, at last, the knowledge of
Where we are standing—
Where we are standing
In this Wonderland
When we rip off all our clothes
And this blind man's patch, veil,
That got tied across our brow.

We are partners straddling the universe.
Someone inside of us
Has one foot
Upon each resplendent pole.
Someone inside of us is now kissing
The hand of God
And wants to share with us
That grand news.

You will find yourself knee-deep in ecstasy
When all your talents to love
Have reached their heights.

Hafiz, time, space, and boredom
Are just passing fads.
All your pain, worry, sorrow
Will someday apologize and confess
They were a great lie.

Let's see,
O yes,
Look how we got distracted,
"Beyond logical events."
I remember we were talking about:
The Ear That Got Sold to a Fish.

It is true
The moon once put a price
Upon my head.
And then hired a gang of
Young thugs.
It seems the Beloved felt
I had been telling too many secrets,
Giving too much of His precious wine
Away for free.

So I got called before a fat burly judge.
But I pleaded my own case well.
I said,

"It is all the fault of prayer,
It has filled me with divine treasures
That I love to loosely spend."

So,
I bought a ticket for my eye
Upon that White Sky Bird
That never touches ground,

And I bribed an ancient deep-sea fish
To buy my ear and drown.

Now whenever the Beloved whispers
Or even slightly moves
I get a scouting report
That a thousand saints could envy
And would pawn their hearts to know.

Hafiz has become
One of the greatest spies upon God
This world has ever seen.

That is why the moon once got rough.
That is why that fat burly judge
Once crowded all of heaven into a small jury box.

God knowingly did risk my case becoming famous
If I won.
I think He really wanted my name
To spread forever wide.

Have you ever contemplated the thought
As I once did,
That the Beloved already knew, already knew,
Everything long before,
So long before we were ever born.

But now to end this drunken song
With its essence in refrain:

Art is the conversation between lovers.

True art awakes the
Extraordinary
Ovation.

AN INFANT IN YOUR ARMS

The tide of my love
Has risen so high let me flood over

You.

Close your eyes for a moment
And maybe all your fears and fantasies

Will end.

If that happened
God would become an infant in your

Arms

And then you
Would have to nurse all

Creation!

FOUR

I Hold the Lion's Paw

I hold the Lion's Paw
Whenever I dance.

I know the ecstasy of the falcon's wings
When they make love against the sky,

And the sun and moon
Sometimes argue over
Who will tuck me in at night.

If you think I am having more fun
Than anyone on this planet
You are absolutely correct.

But Hafiz
Is willing to share all his secrets
About how to befriend God.

Indeed, dear ones,
Hafiz is so very willing
To share all his secrets
About how to know the
Beautiful
One.

I hold the Lion's Paw whenever I dance.

I know the ecstasy of your heart's wings
When they make love against the Sky,

And the sun and moon
Will someday argue over
Who will tuck you in at
Night!

IF THE FALLING OF A HOOF

If the falling of a hoof
Ever rings the temple bells,

If a lonely man's final scream
Before he hangs himself

And the nightingale's perfect lyric
Of happiness
All become an equal cause to dance,

Then the Sun has at last parted
Its curtain before you—

God has stopped playing child's games
With your mind
And dragged you backstage by
The hair,

Shown to you the only possible
Reason

For this bizarre and spectacular
Existence.

Go running through the streets
Creating divine chaos,

Make everyone and yourself ecstatically mad
For the Friend's beautiful open arms.

Go running through this world
Giving love, giving love,

If the falling of a hoof upon this earth
Ever rings the
Temple
Bell.

WHAT THE HELL

The
Real love
I always keep a secret.

All my words
Are sung outside Her window,

For when She lets me in
I take a thousand oaths of silence.

But,
Then She says,

O, then God says,

"What the hell, Hafiz,
Why not give the whole world
My
Address."

SOMEONE UNTIED YOUR CAMEL

I cannot sit still with my countrymen in chains.
I cannot act mute
Hearing the world's loneliness
Crying near the Beloved's heart.

My love for God is such
That I could dance with Him tonight without you,
But I would rather have you there.

Is your caravan lost?

It is,
If you no longer weep from gratitude or happiness,
Or weep
From being cut deep with the awareness
Of the extraordinary beauty
That emanates from the most simple act
And common object.

My dear, is your caravan lost?

It is if you can no longer be kind to yourself
And loving to those who must live
With the sometimes difficult task of loving you.

At least come to know
That someone untied your camel last night
For I hear its gentle voice
Calling for God in the desert.

At least come to know
That Hafiz will always hold a lantern

With galaxies blooming inside
And that

I will always guide your soul to
The divine warmth and exhilaration
Of our Beloved's
Tent.

WHEN I WANT TO KISS GOD

When
No one is looking

I swallow deserts and clouds
And chew on mountains knowing
They are sweet
Bones!

When no one is looking and I want
To kiss
God

I just lift my own hand
To

My

Mouth.

FOR A SINGLE TEAR

I
Know of beauty
That no one has ever
Known.

How could that be possible
When I may seem
So new in infinite time?

It is because God belongs to only you!

Did you hear that?
Did you hear what Hafiz just said?

God belongs to only you!

It is the only reasonable payment
For a single
Tear.

THAT SHAPES THE EYE

Children
Can easily open the
Drawer

That lets the spirit rise up and wear
Its favorite costume of
Mirth and laughter.

When the mind is consumed with
Remembrance of
Him

Something divine happens to the
Heart

That
Shapes the hand and tongue
And eye into
The word
Love.

SO MANY GIFTS

There are so many gifts
Still unopened from your birthday,
There are so many hand-crafted presents
That have been sent to you by God.

The Beloved does not mind repeating,
"Everything I have is also yours."

Please forgive Hafiz and the Friend
If we break into a sweet laughter
When your heart complains of being thirsty
When ages ago
Every cell in your soul
Capsized forever
Into this infinite golden sea.

Indeed,
A lover's pain is like holding one's breath
Too long
In the middle of a vital performance,

In the middle of one of Creation's favorite
Songs.

Indeed, a lover's pain is this sleeping,
This sleeping,
When God just rolled over and gave you
Such a big good-morning kiss!

There are so many gifts, my dear,
Still unopened from your birthday.

O, there are so many hand-crafted presents
That have been sent to your life
From God.

LOVE IS THE FUNERAL PYRE

Love is
The funeral pyre
Where I have laid my living body.

All the false notions of myself
That once caused fear, pain,

Have turned to ash
As I neared God.

What has risen
From the tangled web of thought and sinew

Now shines with jubilation
Through the eyes of angels

And screams from the guts of
Infinite existence
Itself.

Love is the funeral pyre
Where the heart must lay
Its body.

ALLAH, ALLAH, ALLAH

Now

The sky-drum plays

All by itself in my head

Singing all day long

"Allah, Allah,

Allah."

FIVE

Don't Die Again

I am a man
Who knows the ten thousand positions of
Divine love.

I can tell by the light in your eyes
That you are still most familiar
With the few earthly ones,

But would not a good father
Instruct all his heirs
Toward that path that will someday
Deeply satisfy?

This world is a treacherous place
And will surely slay and drown the lazy.

The only life raft here is love
And the Name.

Say it brother,
O, say the divine Name, dear sister,
Silently as you walk.

Don't die again
With that holy ruby mine inside
Still unclaimed

When you could be swinging
A golden pick with
Each
Step.

LIKE A LIFE-GIVING SUN

You could become a great horseman

And help to free yourself and this world

Though only if you and prayer become sweet
Lovers.

It is a naive man who thinks we are not
Engaged in a fierce battle,

For I see and hear brave foot soldiers
All around me going mad,

Falling on the ground in excruciating pain.

You could become a victorious horseman

And carry your heart through this world
Like a life-giving sun

Though only if you and God become sweet
Lovers!

THE GREAT WORK

Love
Is the great work
Though every heart is first an
Apprentice

That slaves beneath the city of Light.

This wondrous trade,
This magnificent throne your soul
Is destined for—

You should not have to think
Much about it,

Is it not clear
An apprentice needs a teacher
Who himself

Has charmed the universe
To reveal its wonders inside his cup.

Happiness is the great work,
Though every heart must first become
A student

To one
Who really knows
About Love.

EFFACEMENT

Effacement
Is a golden gun.
It was not easy to hold it against my head
And fire!

I needed great faith in my master
To suffocate myself
With his holy bag
Full of truth.

I needed great courage
To go out into the dark
Tracking God into the unknown

And not panic or get lost
In all the startling new scents, sounds,
Sights,

Or lose my temper
Tripping on those scheming
Night and day around me.

Hafiz,
Effacement is the emerald dagger
You need to plunge

Deep into yourself upon
This path to divine
Recovery—

Upon this path
To God.

SOME FILL WITH EACH GOOD RAIN

There are different wells within your heart.
Some fill with each good rain,
Others are far too deep for that.

In one well
You have just a few precious cups of water,

That "love" is literally something of yourself,
It can grow as slow as a diamond
If it is lost.

Your love
Should never be offered to the mouth of a
Stranger,

Only to someone
Who has the valor and daring
To cut pieces of their soul off with a knife

Then weave them into a blanket
To protect you.

There are different wells within us.
Some fill with each good rain,

Others are far, far too deep
For that.

THE VINTAGE MAN

The
Difference
Between a good artist
And a great one

Is:

The novice
Will often lay down his tool
Or brush

Then pick up an invisible club
On the mind's table

And helplessly smash the easels and
Jade.

Whereas the vintage man
No longer hurts himself or anyone

And keeps on
Sculpting

Light.

EVERYWHERE

Running
Through the streets
Screaming,

Throwing rocks through windows,
Using my own head to ring
Great bells,

Pulling out my hair,
Tearing off my clothes,

Tying everything I own
To a stick,
And setting it on
Fire.

What else can Hafiz do tonight
To celebrate the madness,
The joy,

Of seeing God
Everywhere!

LIFTS BEYOND CONCEPTION

Independent
Of this body is my mind
When the call from the Golden Nightingale
Lifts and pours my being throughout
The Sky.

Independent of this mind is my
Heart

When God unfurls even a shadow of His tress
Upon my bare shoulder.

Sovereign of my illumined heart

Is the indivisible knowledge
In the gaze of my spirit's wings climbing to
Such a sublime height they each
Become the Sun
Itself

And reside—perched beyond every throne
Known to man.

Hafiz,
This Sufi path of love is so astoundingly
Glorious

That
One day each
Wayfarer upon it will become
The Inconceivable—

The Creator of God
Himself.

GOD'S BUCKET

If this world
Was not held in God's bucket

How could an ocean stand upside down
On its head and never lose a drop?

If your life was not contained in God's cup

How could you be so brave and laugh,
Dance in the face of death?

Hafiz,
There is a private chamber in the soul
That knows a great secret

Of which no tongue can speak.

Your existence my dear, O love my dear,
Has been sealed and marked

"Too sacred," "too sacred," by the Beloved—
To ever end!

Indeed God
Has written a thousand promises
All over your heart

That say,
Life, life, life,
Is far too sacred to
Ever end.

JUST LOOKING FOR TROUBLE

I once had a student
Who would sit alone in his house at night
Shivering with worries
And fears,

And, come morning,
He would often look as though
He had been raped
By a ghost.

Then one day my pity

Crafted for him a knife
From my own divine sword.

Since then,
I have become very proud
Of this student.

For now, come night,
Not only has he lost all his fear,

Now he goes out

Just looking for
Trouble.

The Gift

Our
Union is like this:

You feel cold
So I reach for a blanket to cover
Our shivering feet.

A hunger comes into your body
So I run to my garden
And start digging potatoes.

You ask for a few words of comfort and guidance,
I quickly kneel at your side offering you
This whole book—
As a gift.

You ache with loneliness one night
So much you weep

And I say,

Here's a rope,
Tie it around me,

Hafiz
Will be your companion
For life.

LAUGHING AT THE WORD TWO

Only

That Illumined
One

Who keeps
Seducing the formless into form

Had the charm to win my
Heart.

Only a Perfect One

Who is always
Laughing at the word
Two

Can make you know

Of

Love.

LIFE STARTS CLAPPING

Wherever
God lays His glance
Life starts
Clapping.

The
Myriad
Creatures grab their instruments
And join the
Song.

Whenever love makes itself known
Against another
Body

The
Jewel in the eye starts
To

Dance.

THE FOUNDATION FOR GREATNESS

Greatness

Is always built upon this foundation:

The ability

To appear, speak, and act

As the most

Common

Man.

COURTEOUS TO THE ANT

God

Blooms

From the shoulder

Of the

Elephant

Who becomes

Courteous

To

The

Ant.

HIS WINTER CROP

I have
Seen You heal
A hundred deep wounds with one glance
From Your spectacular eyes,

While your hands, beneath the table,
Pour large bags of salt into the heart-gashes
Of Your most loyal servants.

Dear world, I can offer
An intelligent explanation
For our suffering,
But I hope it really makes sense
To no one here,
And come morning,
You are again at God's door
With ax and pickets,
Eloquent petitions and complaints.

Think of suffering as being washed.
That is to say,
Hafiz, you are often completely soaked
And dripping.

The only advantage I can see in this
In the Friend's long-range plan
Is that when the Beloved bursts
Into ecstatic flames

This whole world will not turn into
A bright oil wick all at once,

Then divine ash,
And ruin His

Winter
Crop.

THE SCENT OF LIGHT

Like a great starving beast

My body is quivering

Fixed

On the scent

Of

Light.

NO CONFLICT

No

Conflict

When the flute is playing

For then I see every movement emanates

From God's

Holy

Dance.

STOP CALLING ME A
PREGNANT WOMAN

My Master once entered a phase
That whenever I would see him
He would say,

"Hafiz,
How did you ever become a pregnant woman?"

And I would reply,

"Dear Attar,
You must be speaking the truth,
But all of what you say is a mystery to me."

Many months passed by in his blessed company.
But one day I lost my patience
Upon hearing that odd refrain
And blurted out,

"Stop calling me a pregnant woman!"

And Attar replied,
"Someday, my sweet Hafiz,
All the nonsense in your brain will dry up
Like a stagnant pool of water
Beneath the sun,

Though if you want to know the Truth
I can so clearly see that God has made love with you
And the whole universe is germinating
Inside your belly

And wonderful words,
Such enlightening words
Will take birth from you

And be cradled against thousands
Of hearts."

A STRANGE FEATHER

All
The craziness,
All the empty plots,
All the ghosts and fears,

All the grudges and sorrows have
Now
Passed.

I must have inhaled
A strange
Feather

That finally

Fell

Out.

I Am Really Just a Tambourine

Good

Poetry

Makes the universe admit a

Secret:

"I am

Really just a tambourine,

Grab hold,

Play me

Against your warm

Thigh."

THE STAIRWAY OF EXISTENCE

We
Are not
In pursuit of formalities
Or fake religious
Laws,

For through the stairway of existence
We have come to God's
Door.

We are
People who need to love, because
Love is the soul's life,

Love is simply creation's greatest joy.

Through
The stairway of existence,
O, through the stairway of existence, Hafiz,

Have
You now come,
Have we all now come to
The Beloved's
Door.

WHAT DO WHITE BIRDS SAY

The earth has disappeared beneath my feet,
It fled from all my ecstasy,

Now like a singing air creature
I feel the Rose
Keep opening.

My heart turned to effulgent wings.
When has love not given freedom?
When has adoration not made one free?

A woman broken in tears and sweat
Stands in a field
Watching the sun and me
Trade jokes.

But never would Hafiz laugh
At your blessed labor
Of finding peace.

What do the dancing white birds say
Looking down upon burnt meadows?

All that you think is rain is not.
Behind the veil Hafiz and angels sometimes weep

Because most eyes are rarely glad
And your divine beauty is still too frightened
To unfurl its thousand swaying arms.

The earth has disappeared beneath my feet,
Illusion fled from all my ecstasy.

Now like a radiant sky creature
God keeps opening,

God keeps opening
Inside of
Me.

HOW DO I LISTEN?

How

Do I

Listen to others?

As if everyone were my Master

Speaking to me

His

Cherished

Last

Words.

THE EARTH BRACES ITSELF

The earth braces itself for the feet
Of a lover of God about to
Dance.

The sky becomes very timid
When a great saint starts waving his arms
In joy,

For the sky knows its prized fixtures,
The sun, moon and planets
Could all wind up
Rolling so wild on the floor!

My dear, this world, its laws,
Our perceptions,
Are such a minute part of existence.

Should not all of our suffering and sadness
Be like this:

As just dropped from an infant's palm
That is asleep against the breast
Of God?

The earth braces itself for the feet of Hafiz.
The sky pulls a mirror from its pocket
And is practicing looking
Coy,

For the Beloved has at last
Opened His arms

And is inviting my heart to eternally
Dance!

The day candle (sun) has forgotten the hour;
The whole world has gone joyously mad.

Look,
The Sun's sweet cheeks are blushing
In the middle of the night

Desiring the rampage of the feet
Of God's lovers.

THE DIFFERENCE BETWEEN

A saintly man and a Perfect One both resided on the
Outskirts of a beautiful city,
Though several miles apart.

One day it came to the attention
Of these two households that a visiting prince
Desired to pay his respects to the most revered spiritual
Leader in that province,
Wanting to gift a small fortune to that man
To help further God's work.

As there had for years been some question
Amongst the population who in fact was
The most spiritual of these two figures,
The prince devised something of a contest,
As he only had time to visit
One of these personages.

The prince sent word:
"In three days I would like to meet with,
In my quarters, the chief representative of each
Of these two renowned religious men
And after questioning them extensively
I and my ministers will then determine
Who in fact of their teachers is the
Closer to God, and thus
To whom we will gift God's own bounty."

The saint upon receiving this news met with
All his close ones. This council discussed the situation
For hours, exploring every nuance,
And considering how much this gold could mean to them.

Then, with a clear majority vote—
Ramjoo was chosen.

Ramjoo was a strikingly young handsome man,
A great hunter, a legendary warrior, a renowned artist.
His intellect was superb, his manners impeccable,
He spoke twenty different languages
And was descended from royal blood himself—
A great-aunt was a queen.
Someone in the saint's camp also knew this prince
Enjoyed the intimate company of men as well as women.
Ramjoo, they all nodded, was the right choice.

The Perfect One upon receiving this "news"
From the prince immediately called for Yasamin;
No consultation with anyone was needed.

Yasamin was a servant woman in the master's
Household.
She was nearly eighty, a famous hag,
And had worked for him all her life—
No one else in the city would hire Yasamin
As she was completely mad
(Perhaps just God-mad), nevertheless her qualifications
For this essential, delicate diplomacy were exact:

She had not combed her hair or bathed for months;
She mostly muttered unintelligible sounds
In her own secret language
That only the master knew.
She often made obscene gestures
While exposing her private regions.

She compulsively picked her nose
And threw boogers with astounding accuracy.

No one had ever known her to go five minutes
Without loudly farting at least four times.
She was psychic, too,
And would probably start beating the prince if
She "saw" he had ever gone too far romantically—
With his camels.

Yasamin, the Perfect One knew,
Was the right choice to be his envoy
Especially when she agreed with a deep enlightened laugh
To add to her already majestic—sublimely free—being
The crown of three live chickens
She would proudly drape over her head
Come the appointed
Royal minute.

The day of the prince came. The two envoys entered
The prince's quarters but were kept separate
And did not even see one another.

Ramjoo went in first
And from behind a door Yasamin could hear singing,
And light lively talk that went on for two hours.

She knew what was happening.
The prince was falling in love with his new guest.

Then Yasamin was brought in
And the prince could not believe his eyes.
He felt tremendously insulted and even became
A bit terrified when, in fact, Yasamin being
Able to "see" into the prince's past,
Started shouting things even he could understand
About that one regrettable night in the desert—

With that young, gorgeous *camel*.
She even hit the prince with two gigantic boogers
From twenty feet away;
Bouncing off his forehead
They both fell right into his tea.

Yasamin was ordered
Beaten and thrown out.

She returned to the master ecstatic
And has never been happier since.

That night the prince could not sleep, but
Finally dozed off for a few minutes just before dawn.
During that short sleep he had this dream:

The Prophet Muhammad
Was seated on a magnificent white horse
And behind the Prophet sat a man smiling wonderfully
At the prince for a moment, before saying,

"Why did you beat my dear Yasamin,
When she spoke only the truth to you?"

The prince bolted awake
And sat up in bed trembling with sweat.

He called for his horse to be saddled
And with ten of his soldiers rode right then
To the saintly man's house pleading to see him.

Upon seeing this man and realizing
He was not the person in the dream,

He then dismissed his soldiers and taking off his shoes,
Weeping now,
Began to walk to the Perfect One's household.

Dear ones,
Use your own storytelling abilities
To end this tale

In a way that will most
Uplift your heart.

THE ANGELS KNOW YOU WELL

You have fathered a child with me.

You had your night of fun.

If You no longer want the love my
Beautiful body can yield

At least take care of that
Holy infant my heart has become.

God, You sired an heir with me
When You gave birth to my soul.

I thought of complaining to all the angels
Last night

About Your treatment of this
"Homeless child,"

But then I remembered they too
Have a long list of love-complaints

Because
They also know You so
Well.

CROOKED DEALS

There is

A madman inside of you

Who is always running for office—

Why vote him in,

For he never keeps the accounts straight.

He gets all kinds of crooked deals

Happening all over town

That will just give you a big headache

And glue to your kisser

A gigantic

Confused

Frown.

THE MILLSTONE'S TALENTS

To the heart's deepest sensibilities
Only the God who created every god
Dares to sing.

In the Tavern
Where the Friend performs
I am amazed

For
There are often vacant seats at night
And the old chairs miss their free dusting
By big, warm rear ends.

The husk on the grain
Needs the Millstone's talents
Before the Royal Eye's intelligence can cure
Life,

And one can see,
See, see that God is everywhere
And whirling.

To your deepest sensibilities my Beloved
Has asked Hafiz to sing
With all of my
Millstone's
Talents.

LET THOUGHT BECOME YOUR BEAUTIFUL LOVER

Let thought become the beautiful Woman.

Cultivate your mind and heart to that depth

That it can give you everything
A warm body can.

Why just keep making love with God's child—
Form

When the Friend Himself is standing
Before us
So open-armed?

My dear,
Let prayer become your beautiful Lover

And become free,
Become free of this whole world
Like Hafiz.

Get the Blame Straight

Understanding the physics of God,
His Indivisible Nature,

Makes every universe and atom confess:

I am just a helpless puppet that cannot dance
Without the movement of His hand.

Dear ones,
This curriculum tonight is for the advanced
And will

Get all the blame straight,

End the mental

Lawsuits

That

Clog

The

Brain—

H
a
l
l
e
l
u
j
a
h

Baby!

REWARDS FOR CLEAR THINKING

Think about this for a second:

God (being God), having Infinite Knowledge,
Not only knew your every thought and action
Your life would ever experience

(Even before you were born)

But He also, being the Divine Creator,
Has etched every moment of your existence
With His own hand

With the precision and care
No artist ever could.

Think about this for a moment:

I have never heard a bird or the sun
Ever say to God,
I am sorry.

There seems to be a great reward
For clear thinking:
All existence is a pawn in the Friend's hands.

Look, one gets wings and gifts to the world
Music each morning;
One turns into such an extraordinary light
He actually becomes a sustainer of a whole planet,

One makes a thousand moons go mad with love
And blush all night

When one can surrender the illusion, the crutch, of
Free will,

Though still live—for the benefit of others—
The highest of moral
Codes.

PLEASE

We are at
The Nile's end.

We are carrying particles
From every continent, creature, and age.

It has been raining on the plains
Of our vision for millions of years

And our senses
Are so muddy compared to Yours—dear God,

But I only hear these words from You
Where we are all trying to embrace
The Clear Sky-Ocean,

"Dear one, come.

Please,
My dear ones,
Come."

THIS CONSTANT YEARNING

We are

Like lutes

Once held by God.

Being away from His warm body

Fully explains

This

Constant

Yearning.

THE SAD GAME

Blame

Keeps the sad game going.

It keeps stealing all your wealth—

Giving it to an imbecile with

No financial skills.

Dear one,

Wise

Up.

THAT REGAL COAT

Joy
Is the royal garment

And now everyday I could wear
That regal
Coat,

But I so love the common man
And feel for all
Their labor

I often paint a vast drop
Of compassion
In

My
Eye.

STOP BEING SO RELIGIOUS

What
Do sad people have in
Common?

It seems
They have all built a shrine
To the past

And often go there
And do a strange wail and
Worship.

What is the beginning of
Happiness?

It is to stop being
So religious

Like

That.

FRIENDS DO THINGS LIKE THIS

Friends do things like this:

Tell which mat their house key is
Hidden under.

Hafiz, jump over, cut right through
All the small talk today:

Look beneath the right-hand corner
Of that Kirman behind
The barn

Where my sweet dog is usually
Sleeping
(Don't worry, she won't bite)

For you would not believe
The extraordinary view
Of God

From my bedroom
Window.

IT FELT LOVE

How
Did the rose
Ever open its heart

And give to this world
All its
Beauty?

It felt the encouragement of light
Against its
Being,

Otherwise,
We all remain

Too

Frightened.

LOOK! I AM A WHALE

We live on the Sun's playground.

Here,
Everyone gets what they want.

Sometimes the body of a beautiful woman,
Sometimes the body of a beautiful man,
Sometimes the body of both
In one.

We used to play that kind of tag
In the animal world too.

Now a mouse,
Now a tiger,
Look! I am a whale—I got tired of the land,
Went back to the ocean for a while.

What power is it in our sinew and mind
That will not die,

That keeps us shopping for the perfect dress?

We have all heard the Flute Player
And keep dancing
Toward Him.

Hafiz,
You have seen the Flute Player
And cannot help but
Whirl.

TWO BEARS

Once
After a hard day's forage
Two bears sat together in silence
On a beautiful vista
Watching the sun go down
And feeling deeply grateful
For life.

Though, after a while
A thought-provoking conversation began
Which turned to the topic of
Fame.

The one bear said,
"Did you hear about Rustam?
He has become famous
And travels from city to city
In a golden cage;

He performs to hundreds of people
Who laugh and applaud
His carnival
Stunts."

The other bear thought for
A few seconds

Then started
Weeping.

THE SKY HUNTER

Keep
Ringing the bell,
Playing the tamboura, calling for Him.

For you
Have touched something holy inside
With your spirit-body
And now your eyes look broken
Without His sacred presence near.

The heart is like that: blessed and ruined
Once it has known
Divine beauty,

Then,
It becomes a restless sky hunter.

The lover keeps circling in their being
Their sweetest moments
With God

Needing to kiss
His face
Again.

FORGIVE THE DREAM

All your images of winter
I see against your sky.

I understand the wounds
That have not healed in you.

They exist
Because God and love
Have yet to become real enough

To allow you to forgive
The dream.

You still listen to an old alley song
That brings your body pain;

Now chain your ears
To His pacing drum and flute.

Fix your eyes upon
The magnificent arch of His brow

That supports
And allows this universe to expand.

Your hands, feet, and heart are wise
And want to know the warmth
Of a Perfect One's circle.

A true saint
Is an earth in eternal spring.

Inside the veins of a petal
On a blooming redbud tree

Are hidden worlds
Where Hafiz sometimes
Resides.

I will spread
A Persian carpet there
Woven with light.

We can drink wine
From a gourd I hollowed
And dried on the roof of my house.

I will bring bread I have kneaded
That contains my own
Divine genes

And cheese from a calf I raised.

My love for your Master is such
You can just lean back
And I will feed you
This truth:

Your wounds of love can only heal
When you can forgive
This dream.

NINE

The Prettiest Mule

Sometimes a mule does not know
What is best for itself.

When the mind is confused like that
It secretly desires a master
With a skilled whip

To guide it to those playgrounds
On the earth's table
Where the Sweet One's light has
Made life more tasty.

Hafiz always carries such a whip
But I rarely need to use it.

I prefer just turning myself into
The prettiest mule
In town

And making my tail sing
Knowing your heart will then
Follow.

TODAY

I
Do not
Want to step so quickly
Over a beautiful line on God's palm
As I move through the earth's
Marketplace
Today.

I do not want to touch any object in this world
Without my eyes testifying to the truth
That everything is
My Beloved.

Something has happened
To my understanding of existence
That now makes my heart always full of wonder
And kindness.

I do not
Want to step so quickly
Over this sacred place on God's body
That is right beneath your
Own foot

As I
Dance with
Precious life
Today.

WISE MEN KEEP TALKING ABOUT

Time is the shop
Where everyone works hard

To build enough love
To break the
Shackle.

Wise men keep talking about
Wanting to meet Her.

Women sometimes pronounce the word God
A little differently:
They can use more feeling and skill
With the heart-lute.

All the world's movements,
Apparent chaos, and suffering I now know happen
In the Splendid Unison:

Our tambourines are striking
The same thigh.

Hafiz stands
At a juncture in this poem.
There are a thousand new wheels I could craft
On a wagon
And place you in—
Lead you to a glimpse of the culture
And seasons in another dimension.

Yet again God
Will have to drop you back at the shop

Where you still have work
With

Love.

BACK INTO HERSELF

A billion times God has turned man
Into Himself.

You stand in line for the
Highest gift
For His generosity cannot end.

But best to bring an instrument along
While waiting in the cold desert

And make some dulcet sounds
To accompany the palms' swaying arms
That are casting silhouettes
Against the sky's curtain
From our fire.

Remind the Friend of your desire
And great patience.

A billion times God has turned man
Back into Herself.

We all stand in line
For the highest
Gift.

THE MULE GOT DRUNK AND
LOST IN HEAVEN

The
Mind is ever a tourist
Wanting to touch and buy new things
Then toss them into an already
Filled closet.

So I craft my words into those guides
That will offer you something fresh
From the Hidden's Tavern.

Few things are stronger than
The mind's need for diverse
Experience.

I am glad
Not many men or women can remain
Faithful lovers to the unreal.

There is a kind of adultery
That God encourages:

Your spirit needs to leave the bed
Of fear.

The gross, the subtle, the mental worlds
Become as a worthless husband.

Women need
To utilize their superior intelligence
About love

So that their hour's legacy
Can make us all stronger and more clement.

Sometimes a poem happens like this one:

The mule I sit on while I recite
Starts off in one direction
But then gets drunk

And lost in
Heaven.

WHY ABSTAIN?

Why
Abstain from love
When like the beautiful snow goose
Someday your soul
Will leave this summer
Camp?

Why
Abstain from happiness
When like a skilled lion
Your heart is
Nearing

And
Will someday see
The divine prey is
Always
Near!

THE WARRIOR

The warriors tame
The beasts in their past
So that the night's hoofs
Can no longer break the jeweled vision
In the heart.

The intelligent and the brave
Open every closet in the future and evict
All the mind's ghosts who have the bad habit
Of barfing everywhere.

For a long time the Universe
Has been germinating in your spine

But only a *Pir** has the talent,
The courage to slay
The past-giant, the future-anxieties.

The warrior
Wisely sits in a circle
With other men
Gathering the strength to unmask
Himself,

Then
Sits, giving,
Like a great illumined planet on
The
Earth.

* Persian: Saint

DIVIDING GOD

The moon starts singing
When everyone is asleep
And the planets throw a bright robe
Around their shoulders and whirl up
Close to her side.

Once I asked the moon,
"Why do you and your sweet friends
Not perform so romantically like that
To a larger crowd?"

And the whole sky chorus resounded,

"The admission price to hear
The lofty minstrels
Speak of love

Is affordable only to those
Who have not exhausted themselves
Dividing God all day
And thus need rest.

The thrilled Tavern fiddlers
Who are perched on the roof

Do not want their notes to intrude
Upon the ears
Where an accountant lives
With a sharp pencil
Keeping score of words
Another

In their great sorrow or sad anger
May have once said
To you."

Hafiz knows:
The sun will stand as your best man
And whistle

When you have found the courage
To marry forgiveness,

When you have found the courage
To marry
Love.

I SAW TWO BIRDS

Both of our mouths
Can fit upon this flute I carry.

My music will sound
So much sweeter that way

With your breath and my breath
Poking each other in the ribs
And kissing.

I saw two birds on a limb this morning
Laughing with the sun.
They reminded me of how
We will one day exist.

My dear,
Keep thinking about God,
Keep thinking about the Beloved
And soon our nest will be the
Whole firmament.

Forget about all your desires for truth,
We have gone far beyond that,
For now it is just—
Pure need.

Both our hearts are meant to sing.
Both our souls are destined to touch
And kiss

Upon this holy flute
God carries.

MUHAMMAD'S TWIN

I

Know

The one you are looking

For.

I call that man Muhammad's

Twin.

You once saw Him, so now your eyes

Are weaving a great net of tenderness

That will one day

Capture

God.

Tiny Gods

Some gods say, the tiny ones,
"I am not here in your vibrant, moist lips
That need to beach themselves upon
The golden shore of a
Naked body."

Some gods say, "I am not
The scarred yearning in the unrequited soul;
I am not the blushing cheek
Of every star and
Planet—

I am not the applauding Chef
Of those precious secretions that can distill
The whole mind into a perfect wincing jewel, if only
For a moment;
Nor do I reside in every pile of sweet warm dung
Born of the earth's
Gratuity."

Some gods say, the ones we need to hang,
"Your mouth is not designed to know His,
Love was not born to consume
The luminous
Realms."

Dear ones,
Beware of the tiny gods frightened men
Create

To bring an anesthetic relief
To their sad
Days.

THIS UNION

This

Union you want

With the earth and sky,

This union we all need with love,

A golden wing from God's heart just

Touched the ground,

Now

Step upon it

With your brave sun-vows

And help our eyes

To

Dance!

WHEN YOU CAN ENDURE

When
The words stop
And you can endure the silence

That reveals your heart's
Pain

Of emptiness
Or that great wrenching-sweet longing,

That is the time to try and listen
To what the Beloved's
Eyes

Most want
To

Say.

THIS TALKING RAG

It
Was all
So clear this morning,

My mind and heart had never felt
More convinced:

There is only God,
A Great Wild
God.

But somehow I got yanked from
That annihilating
Realization

And can now appear again
As this wine-stained
Talking

Rag.

WHO WILL FEED MY CAT?

I

Will need

Someone to feed my cat

When I leave this world,

Though my cat is not ordinary.

She only has three paws:

Fire, air,

Water.

BURGLARS HEAR WATCHDOGS

If one
Is afraid of losing anything
They have not looked into the Friend's eyes;
They have forgotten God's
Promise.

The jewels you get when you meet the Beloved
Go on multiplying themselves;
They take root
Everywhere.

They keep mating all the time
Like spring-warmed
Creatures.

Burglars
Hear watchdogs inside of His
Gifts

And run.

A STILL CUP

For

God

To make love,

For the divine alchemy to work,

The Pitcher needs a still cup.

Why

Ask Hafiz to say

Anything more about

Your most

Vital

Requirement?

THAT LAMP THAT NEEDS NO OIL

I have made the journey into Nothing.
I have lit that lamp that
Needs no oil.

I have cried great streams
Of emerald crystals
On my scarred knees, begging love

To never again let me hear from
Any world

The sound of my own name,
Even from the voice of divine thought

Or see that pen you gave me, God,
In the sun's or sky's skillful hand
Writing
Anything other than the word—
One.

I have made the journey into Nothing.
I have become that flame that needs
No fuel.

Beloved,
Now what need is there to ever
Call for Hafiz?

For if you did,
I would just step out
of *You.*

TOO WONDERFUL

No one could ever paint
A too wonderful
Picture

Of my heart
Or
God.

ELEVEN

Elephant Wondering

A seed
Has sprouted beneath a golden leaf
In a dark forest.

This seed is seriously contemplating,
Seriously wondering about
The moseying habits
Of the Elephant.

Why?

Because
In this lucid, wine-drenched tale
The Elephant is really—
God,

Who has His big foot upon us,
Upon the golden leaf under which lies
This sprouting
Universe

Wherein
We are all a little concerned
And

Nervous.

AN OLD MUSICIAN

How
Should
Those who know of God
Meet and
Part?

The way
An old musician
Greets his beloved
Instrument

And will take special care,
As a great artist always does,

To enhance the final note
Of each

Performance.

THE FISH AND I WILL CHAT

Once
In a while
The fish and I will chat
In the silent
Language:

We look
Into each other's eyes and smile,
And they often
Say,

"Hey, Hafiz
We see you know the joy of
Our existence,

We see you have discovered how meditation
Can free you from land,
Mind, debts, alimony—the
Whole works,

And like
Us

Let you carouse all day
In

God."

THE HEART IS RIGHT

The
Heart is right to cry

Even when the smallest drop of light,
Of love,
Is taken away.

Perhaps you may kick, moan, scream
In a dignified
Silence,

But you are so right
To do so in any fashion

Until God returns
To

You.

OUT OF GOD'S HAT

The stars got poured into the sky
Out of a Magician's hat last night,
And all of them have fallen into my hair.
Some have even tangled my eyelashes
Into luminous, playful knots.

Wayfarer,
You are welcome to cut a radiant tress
That lays upon my shoulders.
Wrap it around your trembling heart and body
That craves divine comfort and warmth.

I am like a pitcher of milk
In the hands of a mother who loves you.

All of my contents now
Have been churned into dancing suns and moons.

Lean your sweet neck and mouth
Out of that dark nest where you hide,
I will pour effulgence into your mind.

Come spring
You can find me rolling in fields
That are exploding in
Holy battles

Of scents, of sounds—everything is
A brilliant colored nova on a stem.

Forest animals hear me laughing
And surrender their deepest instincts and fears,

They come charging into meadows
To lick my hands and face,

This makes me so happy,
I become so happy

That my rising wink turns into a magic baton.
When my soft-eyed creatures see that wonderful signal
We all burst into singing

And make strange and primal beautiful sounds!

My only regret in this world then becomes:

That your shyness keeps you from placing
Your starving body against God

And seeing the Beloved become so pleased
With your courage

That His belly begins to rock and rock,
Then more planets get to leap
Onto the welcome mat of existence
All because
Of your precious love.

The Friend has turned my verse into sacred pollen.
When a breeze comes by

Falcons and butterflies
And playful gangs of young angels
Mounted on emerald spears

Take flight from me like a great sandstorm
That can blind you to all but the Truth!

Dear one,
Even if you have no net to catch Venus

My music
Will circle this earth for hundreds of years
And fall like resplendent debris,
Holy seed, onto a fertile woman.

For Hafiz
Wants to help you laugh at your every
Desire.

Hafiz
Wants you to know

Your life within God's arms,
Your dance within God's
Arms

Is already

Perfect!

THE CLAY BOWL'S DESTINY

The
Ship you are riding on,
Look where it is
Heading:

Your body's port is the graveyard.

Realizing the destiny of each clay bowl
Tossed into the sky
With no one to
Catch it

I finally
Accepted the Beloved's kind offer
To enroll

In
His sublime,
Ball-busting course
Of
Spirit
Love.

I HOPE YOU WON'T SUE
THIS OLD MAN

I have
Nothing to say
For God has taken His sharp knife
And completely
Hollowed me,

Yet a mysterious wind comes by
And moves the Invisible.

I enter your soul.
Your beauty, dear pilgrim, startles me,
Causes my spirit's foot to slip

Against one of the lute strings on
Your heart.

Then Hafiz just translates
The cries of your love
As if they were
My own
Words.

I hope
You won't sue
This drunk Old Man
For
That.

FAITHFUL LOVER

The moon came to me last night
With a sweet question.

She said,

"The sun has been my faithful lover
For millions of years.

Whenever I offer my body to him
Brilliant light pours from his heart.

Thousands then notice my happiness
And delight in pointing
Toward my beauty.

Hafiz,
Is it true that our destiny
Is to turn into Light
Itself?"

And I replied,

Dear moon,
Now that your love is maturing,
We need to sit together
Close like this more often

So I might instruct you
How to become
Who you
Are!

NOW IS THE TIME

Now is the time to know
That all that you do is sacred.

Now, why not consider
A lasting truce with yourself and God.

Now is the time to understand
That all your ideas of right and wrong
Were just a child's training wheels
To be laid aside
When you can finally live
With veracity
And love.

Hafiz is a divine envoy
Whom the Beloved
Has written a holy message upon.

My dear, please tell me,
Why do you still
Throw sticks at your heart
And God?

What is it in that sweet voice inside
That incites you to fear?

Now is the time for the world to know
That every thought and action is sacred.

This is the time
For you to deeply compute the impossibility

That there is anything
But Grace.

Now is the season to know
That everything you do
Is sacred.

Counting Moles

Lovers
Don't tell all of their
Secrets.

They might
Count each other's moles
That reside in the shy
Regions,

Then keep that tally strictly
To themselves.

God and I
Have signed a contract
To be even more intimate than
That!

Though a clause
Mentions

Something about not drawing detailed maps
To all His beautiful

Laughing
Moles.

❊

HAFIZ

It

Is all

Just a love contest

And I never

Lose.

Now you have another good reason

To spend more time

With

Me.

THE BODY A TREE

The body a tree.
God a wind.

When He moves me like this,
Like this,

Angels bump heads with each other
Gathering beneath my cheeks,
Holding their wine
Barrels

Catching the brilliant tear,
Pearl

Rain.

A GREAT NEED

Out

Of a great need

We are all holding hands

And climbing.

Not loving is a letting go.

Listen,

The terrain around here

Is

Far too

Dangerous

For

That.

THERE COULD BE HOLY FALLOUT

We are often in battle.
So often defending every side of the fort,
It may seem, all alone.

Sit down, my dear,
Take a few deep breaths,
Think about a loyal friend.
Where is your music,
Your pet, a brush?

Surely one who has lasted as long as you
Knows some avenue or place inside
That can give a sweet respite.

If you cannot slay your panic,
Then say within
As convincingly as you can,
"It is all God's will!"

Now pick up your life again.
Let whatever is out there
Come charging in,

Laugh and spit into the air,
There could be holy fallout.

Throw those ladders like tiny match sticks
With "just" phantoms upon them
Who might be trying to scale your heart.

Your love has an eloquent tone.
The sky and I want to hear it!

If you still feel helpless
Give our battle cry again,

Hafiz
Has shouted it a myriad times,

"It is all,
It is all the Beloved's will!"

What is that luminous rain I see
All around you in the future

Sweeping in from the east plain?

It looks like, O it looks like
Holy fallout

Filling your mouth and palms
With Joy!

TRYING TO WEAR PANTS

You are
A royal fish
Trying to wear pants
In a country as foreign
As land.

Now there's a problem
Worth discussing.

Your separation from God has ripened.
Now fall like a golden fruit
Into my hand.

All your wounds from craving love
Exist because of heroic deeds.

Now trade in those medals;
That courage will help this world.

One needs to love those they have yet to love
To stand near the Friend.

Why
Be a royal fish
Trying to wear pants?

Hafiz,
What are you talking about?
Has something happened to your once
Brilliant
Mind?

THIS SKY

This

Sky

Where we live

Is no place to lose your wings

So love, love,

Love.

IT IS UNANIMOUS

It is unanimous where I come from.
Everyone agrees on one thing:

It's no fun
When God is not near.

All are hunters.
The wise man learns the Friend's weaknesses
And sets a clever trap.

Listen,
The Beloved has agreed to play a game
Called
Love.

Our sun sat in the sky
Way before this earth was born
Waiting to caress a billion faces.

Hafiz encourages all art

For at its height it brings Light near
To us.

The wise man learns what draws God
Near.

It is the beauty of compassion
In your heart.

TWO PUDDLES CHATTING

It rained during the night
And two puddles formed in the dark
And began chatting.
One said,

"It is so nice to at last be upon this earth
And to meet you as well,

But what will happen when
The brilliant Sun comes
And turns us back into spirit again?"

Dear ones,
Enjoy the night as much as you can.

Why ever trouble your heart with flight,
When you have just arrived
And your body is so full of warm desires.
And look:

So many meadows of soft hair are
Planted upon you.

Why ever trouble yourself with God
When He is so unjudging
And kind

Unless you are blessed and live
Near the circle of a
Perfect One?

HIS BALLET COMPANY

Everything
Of
Intelligence

Innocently watches the way

One manages their body
And silver.

One's care of form
Is as

A
Divine
Audition to

The Firmament's Ballet
Company.

THIRTEEN

Reverence

Because
There is nothing
Outside of my Master's body

I try
To show reverence
To all things.

Because
There is nothing
Inside of my Master's body

I am saved
From all reason
And surrender understanding.

No wonder, Hafiz,
It has been
Unusual

For a smile to forsake
You!

THAT TREE WE PLANTED

Beloved Master

That tree we planted near the spot
That became your
Tomb

Has grown so well
That it is now several times
My height.

When
The season comes
That makes its leaves bow
And whirl,

Hafiz
Will then sleep upon the ground
Hoping in at least
A dream

You
Will kiss my cheek
Again!

I VOTE FOR YOU FOR GOD

When your eyes have found the strength
To constantly speak to the world
All that is most dear
To your own
Life,

When your hands, feet, and tongue
Can perform in that rare unison
That comforts this longing earth
With the knowledge

Your soul,
Your soul has been groomed
In His city of love;

And when you can make others laugh
With jokes
That belittle no one
And your words always unite,

Hafiz
Does vote for you.

Hafiz will vote for you to be
The minister of every country in
This universe.

Hafiz does vote for you my dear.
I vote for you
To be
God.

A ONE-STORY HOUSE

I am glad that my Master lived
In a one-story
House

When I began to traverse
The early stages of
Love.

For when he would speak
Of the wonders and the beauty of creation,

When he began to reveal
The magnificent realities of God

I could not control my happiness
And would commence
An ecstatic dance

That most always resulted in a
Tremendous encore—

A dive, head first,
Out of his
Window.

Hafiz,
The Friend was very kind to you
During those early years

And you only broke your big nose
Seventeen times!

THE GREAT RELIGIONS

The
Great religions are the
Ships,

Poets the life
Boats.

Every sane person I know has jumped
Overboard.

That is good for business
Isn't it

Hafiz?

WHAT HAPPENS TO THE GUEST

The hand sat in the classroom
Of the eye

And soon learned to love
Beauty.

The sky sat in the classroom
Of God

And now look what it gives us at night:
All that it learned.

There was a time when man
Was so burdened with survival
That he rarely bathed in dancing sounds.

But dear ones,
Now drop your pointed shields that wound.

What happens to the guest who visits the house
Of a great musician?

Of course his tastes become refined.

There are some who can visit
That Luminous Sphere that reveals
This life never
Was,

The truth of that experience
Is reserved for so
Very few;

God draws back like a kite
Some of those who get lost in the Sun

And after their recovery
From being sublimely independent,
Having known the Unspeakable Union—

They might try again with all their courage
To sing a simple tune like this:

"What happens to the guests who keep visiting
The verse of a Perfect One?

Their voices and cells become refined
And like the soft night candle (the moon)

They begin to give to this world
All the light they have
Learned."

Your hand sits in the classroom
Of God,

An apprentice as Hafiz was,
Mastering the craft of
Divine beauty

As this earth spins on
The Potter's
Wheel.

I WANT BOTH OF US

I want both of us
To start talking about this great love

As if you, I, and the Sun were all married
And living in a tiny room,

Helping each other to cook,
Do the wash,
Weave and sew,
Care for our beautiful
Animals.

We all leave each morning
To labor on the earth's field.
No one does not lift a great pack.

I want both of us to start singing like two
Traveling minstrels
About this extraordinary existence
We share,

As if
You, I, and God were all married

And living in
A tiny
Room.

LIKE PASSIONATE LIPS

There are
So many positions of
Love:

Each curve on a branch,

The thousand different ways
Your eyes can embrace us,

The infinite shapes your
Mind can draw,

The spring
Orchestra of scents,

The currents of light combusting
Like passionate lips,

The revolution of Existence's skirt
Whose folds contain other worlds,

Your every sigh that falls against
His inconceivable
Omnipresent
Body.

CUCUMBERS AND PRAYERS

All day long
The earth shouts
"Gee, thanks."

Such an exuberant gee,
It starts throwing
Things

As if God were passing by in a parade encouraging
Rowdy behavior
By looking so beautiful—
That a whole avalanche of mania swoops in!

I like this idea of throwing things at God,
And especially—His making us rowdy!

Thus, as soon as Hafiz is out of bed
I start stuffing large sacks
With old shoes, cucumbers,
And
Prayers

For the upcoming
Consecrated

Free-for-all—
And who knows
What else.

A Cushion for Your Head

Just sit there right now
Don't do a thing
Just rest.

For your separation from God,
From love,

Is the hardest work
In this
World.

Let me bring you trays of food
And something
That you like to
Drink.

You can use my soft words
As a cushion
For your
Head.

THESE BEAUTIFUL LOVE GAMES

Young lovers wisely say,

"Let's try it from this angle,
Maybe something marvelous will happen,

Maybe three suns and two moons
Will roll out
From a hiding place in the body
Our passion has yet to ignite."

Old lovers say,
"We can do it one more time,
How about from this longitude
And latitude—

Swinging from a rope tied to the ceiling,

Maybe a part of God
Is still hiding in a corner of your heart
Our devotion has yet to reveal."

Bottom line:

Do not stop playing
These beautiful
Love
Games.

THE BAG LADY

I am the bag lady in every city,

I have a spot on every street.

My sacks are full of holiness

So I have come to peddle,
To touch your feet.

I give Myself
To Myself on rare occasions because
I am so very shy.

Hafiz, the monarchs of this world
Are but slaves to thee

Since the Beloved took His seat
In your eye.

I am the bag lady in every city.
I am playing divine music in every world.

My sacks are full of holiness.
I am asking,

May I please bow
To you.

THE AMBIENCE OF LOVE

We all
Sit in His orchestra,
Some play their
Fiddles,

Some wield their
Clubs.

Tonight is worthy of music.

Let's get loose
With
Compassion,

Let's drown in the delicious
Ambience of
Love.

TIRED OF SPEAKING SWEETLY

Love wants to reach out and manhandle us,
Break all our teacup talk of God.

If you had the courage and
Could give the Beloved His choice, some nights,
He would just drag you around the room
By your hair,
Ripping from your grip all those toys in the world
That bring you no joy.

Love sometimes gets tired of speaking sweetly
And wants to rip to shreds
All your erroneous notions of truth

That make you fight within yourself, dear one,
And with others,

Causing the world to weep
On too many fine days.

God wants to manhandle us,
Lock us inside of a tiny room with Himself
And practice His dropkick.

The Beloved sometimes wants
To do us a great favor:

Hold us upside down
And shake all the nonsense out.

But when we hear
He is in such a "playful drunken mood"

Most everyone I know
Quickly packs their bags and hightails it
Out of town.

A ROOT IN EACH ACT
AND CREATURE

The sun's eyes are painting fields again.

Its lashes with expert strokes
Are sweeping across the land.

A great palette of light has embraced
This earth.

Hafiz, if just a little clay and water
Mixed in His bowl
Can yield such exquisite scents, sights,
Music—and whirling forms—

What unspeakable wonders must await with
The commencement of unfolding
Of the infinite number of petals
That are the
Soul.

What excitement will renew your body
When we all begin to see
That His heart resides in
Everything?

God has a root in each act and creature
That He draws His mysterious
Divine life from.

His eyes are painting fields again.

The Beloved with His own hands is tending,
Raising like a precious child,
Himself in
You.

OUR HEARTS SHOULD
DO THIS MORE

I sit in the streets with the homeless

My clothes stained with the wine
From the vineyards the saints tend.

Light has painted all acts
The same color

So I sit around and laugh all day
With my friends.

At night if I feel a divine loneliness
I tear the doors off Love's mansion

And wrestle God onto the floor.

He becomes so pleased with Hafiz
And says,

"Our hearts should do this more."

TURN LEFT A THOUSAND FEET
FROM HERE

What I really want to give you
I can't,

Yet all day long
I try painting maps on the sky
With bright, tender sounds

That say,

"Turn left a thousand feet from here,
Just past that next hill.

Then make a sharp right
As soon as you see that big rock
That looks like an egg,
There you will find a decent tavern."

I am like a wise friend.
If you come close to me

I will write down the address
Of the Woman who will ravish you most.

Hafiz never wants to offend,

So in anything I ever say
You can always freely switch the gender.

Come close to me,
I will whisper in your ear

A secret about the One who
Has made us all
Nuts.

IMAGINATION DOES NOT EXIST

You should come close to me tonight wayfarer
For I will be celebrating you.

Your beauty still causes me madness,
Keeps the neighbors complaining
When I start shouting in the middle of the night
Because I can't bear all this joy.

I will be giving birth to suns.
I will be holding forests upside down
Gently shaking soft animals from trees and burrows
Into my lap.

What you conceive as imagination
Does not exist for me.

Whatever you can do in a dream
Or on your mind-canvas

My hands can pull—alive—from my coat pocket.

But let's not talk about my divine world,

For what I most want to know
Tonight is:

All about
You.

THROW ME ON A SCALE

Today love has completely gutted me.
I am lying in the market like a
Filleted grouper,

Speechless,
Every desire and sinew absolutely silent
But I am still so fresh.

Everything is now the same to me.
Listen:

The touch of a beautiful woman
As she lifts me near,
Drawing my scent into her body;
She thinks about taking me home.

The touch of a wondrous fly
Drinking my vital fluids
Through a strange shaped flute,

The sun laying its radiant gaze against my cheek,
Human voices and the breeze from a passing
Horse's tail,

All send miraculous currents into
My world.

God's beauty has split me wide open.
Throw Hafiz on a scale,
Wrap me in cloth,
Bring me home.

Lift a piece of my knowledge to your lips
So I can melt inside of you
And sing.

THE HATCHECK GIRL

Why
Are there
So few in the court
Of a perfect
Saint?

Because
Every time you are near Him
You have to leave pieces
Of your
Ego

With
The hatcheck
Girl

Who won't give them
Back—

O
O
O
U
C
H
.

DAMN THIRSTY

First
The fish needs to say,

"Something ain't right about this
Camel ride—

And I'm
Feeling so damn

Thirsty."

Two Giant Fat People

God

And I have become

Like two giant fat people

Living in a

Tiny boat.

We

Keep

Bumping into each other and

L
a
u
g
h
i
n
g
.

SCRATCHING MY BACK

You
Can think of Hafiz as a divine
Old dog

Who just keeps scratching his back
On the Moon.

O, I don't care about your thoughts
Or what you have ever done,

Just open up this book whenever you are
Sad

For I love the way you
Smile!

IF YOU DON'T STOP THAT

I used to live in
A cramped house with confusion
And pain.

But then I met the Friend
And started getting drunk
And singing all
Night.

Confusion and pain
Started acting nasty,
Making threats,
With talk like this,

"If you don't stop 'that'—
All that fun—

We're
Leaving."

ELEGANCE

It
Is not easy
To stop thinking ill
Of others.

Usually one must enter into a friendship
With a person

Who has accomplished that great feat himself.
Then

Something
Might start to rub off on you
Of that

True
Elegance.

A HOLE IN A FLUTE

I am

A hole in a flute

That the Christ's breath moves through—

Listen to this

Music.

I am the concert

From the mouth of every

Creature

Singing with the myriad

Chords.

✳

UNTIL

I think we are frightened every

Moment of our lives

Until we

Know

Him.

WHY AREN'T WE SCREAMING DRUNKS?

The sun once glimpsed God's true nature
And has never been the same.

Thus that radiant sphere
Constantly pours its energy
Upon this earth
As does He from behind
The veil.

With a wonderful God like that
Why isn't everyone a screaming drunk?

Hafiz's guess is this:

Any thought that you are better or less
Than another man

Quickly
Breaks the wine
Glass.

DROPPING KEYS

The small man

Builds cages for everyone

He

Knows.

While the sage,

Who has to duck his head

When the moon is low,

Keeps dropping keys all night long

For the

Beautiful

Rowdy

Prisoners.

ALL THE TALENTS OF GOD

All the talents of God are within you.

How could this be otherwise
When your soul
Derived from His
Genes!

I love that expression,
"All the talents of God are within you."

Sometimes Hafiz cannot help but to applaud
Certain words that rise from my depths

Like the scent of a lover's
Body.

Hold this book close to your heart
For it contains wonderful
Secrets.

THE GREAT EXPANSE

Anger

Sinks the boat.

Now we are not praising

That "drowning" in His ocean,

Just crossing the great expanse

Of each minute with all the compassion and

Dignity we can

Find.

I IMAGINE NOW FOR AGES

It
Happened
Again last
Night:

Love
Popped the cork on itself—
Splattered my brains
Across the
Sky.

I imagine now for ages
Something of Hafiz
Will appear

To fall like
Stars.

Spiced Manna

Someone
Will steal you if you don't
Stay near,

And sell you as a slave in the
Market.

I sing
To the nightingales' hearts
Hoping they will learn
My verse

So that no one will ever imprison
Your brilliant angel
Feathers.

Have I put enough spiced manna
On your plate
Tonight

In this Tavern
Where Hafiz
Serves?

If not please wait
For more light is now
Fermenting.

Someone will steal you if you
Don't stay near,

And sell you as a slave in
The market,

So your Beloved and I
Sing.

A HARD DECREE

Last

Night

God
Posted
On the Tavern wall

A hard decree for all of love's inmates

Which read:

If your heart cannot find a joyful work

The jaws of this world
Will probably

Grab hold of your

Sweet
Ass.

AND FOR NO REASON

And
For no reason
I start skipping like a child.

And
For no reason
I turn into a leaf
That is carried so high
I kiss the Sun's mouth
And dissolve.

And
For no reason
A thousand birds
Choose my head for a conference table,
Start passing their
Cups of wine
And their wild songbooks all around.

And
For every reason in existence
I begin to eternally,
To eternally laugh and love!

When I turn into a leaf
And start dancing,
I run to kiss our beautiful Friend
And I dissolve in the Truth
That I Am.

SOMETIMES I SAY TO A POEM

Sometimes I say to a poem,

"Not now,
Can't you see I am bathing!"

But the poem usually doesn't care
And quips,

"Too bad, Hafiz,
No getting lazy—

You promised God you would help out

And He just came up with this
New tune."

Sometimes I say to a poem,

"I don't have the strength
To wring out another drop
Of the Sun."

And the poem will often
Respond

By climbing onto a barroom table:

Then lifts its skirt, winks,
Causing the whole sky to
Fall.

THE SUBURBS

Complaint
Is only possible

While living in the suburbs
Of God.

SHE RESPONDED

The birds' favorite songs
You do not hear,

For their most flamboyant music takes place
When their wings are stretched
Above the trees

And they are smoking the opium
Of pure freedom.

It is healthy for the prisoner
To have faith

That one day he will again move about
Wherever he wants,
Feel the wondrous grit of life—
Less structured,

Find all wounds, debts stamped canceled,
Paid.

I once asked a bird,
"How is it that you fly in this gravity
Of darkness?"

She responded,

"Love lifts
Me."

WE MIGHT HAVE TO MEDICATE YOU

Resist your temptation to lie
By speaking of separation from God,

Otherwise,
We might have to medicate
You.

In the ocean
A lot goes on beneath your eyes.

Listen,
They have clinics there too
For the insane
Who persist in saying things like:

"I am independent from the
Sea,

God is not always around

Gently
Pressing against
My body."

THE IDIOT'S WAREHOUSE

I know the idiot's warehouse
Is always full.

I know each of us
Could run back and forth from there
All day long

And show everyone our vast collection.

Though tonight, Hafiz,
Retire from the madness for an hour,

Gather with some loyal friends
Or sit alone

And
Sing beautiful songs

To God.

WHEN YOU WAKE

Wayfarer,
We are like two cups of water
That God poured in a vase.

I am one with you beyond
Recognition.

Of course
Whatever dreams
You have of this world
I can also say are mine.

Odd,
But it is true,

"Water" can sleep.

When you wake, dear one,
Do not be frightened,

We will be swinging a rope
Around Muhammad,

Watching the Sun
So joyously laugh and skip

In the middle of our Unbelievable
Divine

Union!

THIS TEACHING BUSINESS
ISN'T EASY

The most
Difficult task in hunting you, God,

Is using those arrows and bow
You gave my heart.

They are made of plain water I aim
A great distance
At the Sun.

Hafiz, who can understand
The profound absurdity of all effort
On this
Path.

Why not state this ancient dilemma
From another view.

Listen:
Not once in our history
Has an ant gone out and captured
An elephant single-handed.

Does that tell you anything new?
Maybe not.

This teaching business
Isn't
Easy.

THE MOUNTAIN GOT TIRED
OF SITTING

The sun
Won a beauty contest and became a jewel
Set upon God's right hand.

The earth agreed to be a toe ring on the
Beloved's foot
And has never regretted its decision.

The mountains got tired
Of sitting amongst a sleeping audience

And are now stretching their arms
Toward the Roof.

The clouds gave my soul an idea
So I pawned my gills
And rose like a winged diamond

Ever trying to be near
More love, more love
Like you.

The Mountain got tired of sitting
Amongst a snoring crowd inside of me
And rose like a ripe sun
Into my eye.

My soul gave my heart a brilliant idea
So Hafiz is rising like a
Winged diamond.

Where Is the Door to the Tavern?

Where is the door to God?

In the sound of a barking dog,

In the ring of a hammer,

In a drop of rain,

In the face of

Everyone

I see.

BECOMING HUMAN

Once a man came to me and spoke for hours about
"His great visions of God" he felt he was having.

He asked me for confirmation, saying,
"Are these wondrous dreams true?"

I replied, "How many goats do you have?"

He looked surprised and said,
"I am speaking of sublime visions
And you ask
About goats!"

And I spoke again saying,
"Yes, brother—how many do you have?"

"Well, Hafiz, I have sixty-two."

"And how many wives?"
Again he looked surprised, then said,
"Four."

"How many rose bushes in your garden,
How many children,
Are your parents still alive,
Do you feed the birds in winter?"

And to all he answered.

Then I said,
"You asked me if I thought your visions were true,

I would say that they were if they make you become
More human,

More kind to every creature and plant
That you know."

IN NEED OF THE BREATH

My heart
Is an unset jewel
Upon the tender night
Yearning for its dear old friend
The Moon.

When the Nameless One debuts again
Ten thousand facets of my being unfurl wings
And reveal such a radiance inside
I enter a realm divine—
I too begin to so sweetly cast light,
Like a lamp,
Through the streets of this
World.

My heart is an unset jewel
Upon existence
Waiting for the Friend's touch.

Tonight
My heart is an unset ruby
Offered bowed and weeping to the Sky.

I am dying in these cold hours
For the resplendent glance of God.

I am dying
Because of a divine remembrance
Of who—I really am.

Hafiz, tonight,
Your soul
Is a brilliant reed instrument

In need of the breath of the
Christ.

THE HEART'S CORONATION

The pawn

Always sits stunned,

Chained, unable to move

Beneath God's magnificent power.

It is essential for the heart's coronation

For the pawn to realize

There is nothing but divine movement

In this

World.

THE THOUSAND-STRINGED
INSTRUMENT

The heart is
The thousand-stringed instrument.

Our sadness and fear come from being
Out of tune with love.

All day long God coaxes my lips
To speak,

So that your tears will not stain
His green dress.

It is not that the Friend is vain,
It is just your life we care about.

Sometimes the Beloved
Takes my pen in hand,
For Hafiz is just a simple man.

The other day the Old One
Wrote on the Tavern wall:

"The heart is
The thousand-stringed instrument

That can only be tuned with
Love."

THEN WINKS

Everything is clapping today,

Light,
Sound,
Motion,
All movement.

A rabbit I pass pulls a cymbal
From a hidden pocket
Then winks.

This causes a few planets and I
To go nuts
And start grabbing each other.

Someone sees this,
Calls a
Shrink,

Tries to get me
Committed
For
Being too
Happy.

Listen: this world is the lunatic's sphere,
Don't always agree it's real,

Even with my feet upon it
And the postman knowing my door

My address is somewhere else.

AND THEN YOU ARE

And then You are like this:

A small bird decorated
With orange patches of light
Waving your wings near my window,

Encouraging me with all of existence's love—
To dance.

And then You are like this:

A cruel word that stabs me
From the mouth of a strange costume You wear;
A guise You had too long tricked me into thinking
Could be other—than You.

And then You are . . .

The firmament
That spins at the end of a string in Your hand
That You offer to mine saying,
"Did you drop this—surely
This is yours."

And then You are, O then You are:

The Beloved of every creature
Revealed with such grandeur—bursting
From each cell in my body,
I kneel, I laugh,
I weep, I sing,
I sing.

THE INTELLIGENT MAN

The intelligent man quickly realizes

The impotence of

Gold.

THE CHORUS IN THE EYE

Your eye has a melody we want to hear.
God rises from a tuned instrument.

The sun and moon
Will gladly wear robes

And sway as playful children
When the *Pir** directs Light.

Hafiz,
Could you slip magic into sounds
Then pour them
Into the earth's bruised ear?

Hafiz, could you whisper the luminous
Close to each wayfarer's body
And let the whole world know
About the Beloved's
True nature?

Yes, dear ones, I can,
Listen to one of my favorite words
That the Friend too is always saying to us:
Mashuq, Mashuq
(Sweetheart).

The chorus in the heart needs to sing.

Love is sovereign and ceaselessly moves

*Persian: saint

From the tuned clay drum,

Chanting, humming all day long, *Mashuq,*
Mashuq to everything.

FIND A BETTER JOB

Now

That

All your worry

Has proved such an

Unlucrative

Business,

Why

Not

Find a better

Job.

THE LUTE WILL BEG

You need to become a pen
In the Sun's hand.

We need for the earth to sing
Through our pores and eyes.

The body will again become restless
Until your soul paints all its beauty
Upon the sky.

Don't tell me, dear ones,
That what Hafiz says is not true,

For when the heart tastes its glorious destiny
And you awake to our constant need
For your love

God's lute will beg
For your
Hands.

When the Sun Conceived a Man

What could Hafiz utter about that day
When the Sun conceived a Man,
Gave birth to Itself
As Reality and Truth?

What justice could all the speech in creation
Ever say
About that resplendent morning
When the Eternal Handsome One
Let His face
Reappear by grace in form?

There is something I have seen
In the interior of Muhammad
That is the luminous root
Of all existence,
Independent of space and time's
Novice dance
Across a single lute string
Of the Infinite.

What can even the love of Hafiz express
For the Ancient Sweet Man
Who forever begets compassion
And divine playfulness?

What can the vortex of my sublime wit,
Insight, and gratitude ever say
About the Father of the Perfect Ones,
When they, themselves,
Can turn you into God?

I carry gifts today
From the kings of fish, beasts, birds,
And angels.

I carry gifts today
From rivers, seas, fields, stars,
And from every soul,
From every soul—
That will ever
Be!

Beloved
Let us know
What light first saw and said
When it discovered
You,

Then leaped and swooned
In such a wonderful laughter
That light became
This earthen floor
And sky.

O, Eternal One,
On this ever present holy day
Forget your divine reserve—

Throw wide the Tavern doors.

Give all your thirsty loyal rogues
A drink of your sacred vintage,
Free us from ourselves a while

With the blessed consuming knowledge
Of your Omnipresent Being.

We are your yearning brides, why hide it?
We are singed dervish moths.
Our souls know
Of that immaculate fire you keep
That belongs to us!

Even death now will have no power
To quiet your Name
From beating wildly in our hearts.

Wayfarer,
Now is no time to sit still

For nothing but a great clamor of joy
And music

Can make any sense
Today!

A MIME

A mime stands upon a gallows
For a crime he did not do.
When given a last chance to speak,
He remains true to his art.

A crowd of hundreds has gathered
To see his last performance,
Knowing he will not talk.

The mime takes from the sky
The circles of bright spheres,
Lays them on a table,
Expressing deep love
For the companionship and guidance
They have given him for so many years.

He brings the seas before our eyes,
Somehow a golden fin appears, splashes.
Look, dear ones, there is turquoise rain.

He removes his heart from his body and seems to
Arouse all life on this splendid earth
With such a sacred tenderness,
There for an extraordinary moment
It looked like someone was giving birth
To the Christ again.

He mounts his soul upon the body of Freedom.
The great Breeze comes by.
The sun and moon join hands,
They bow so gracefully

That for a moment, for a moment
Everyone knows that God is real,

So the tongue fell out
Of the mouth of this world
For days.

THE QUINTESSENCE
OF LONELINESS

I am like a heroin addict
In my longing for a sublime state,

For that ground of Conscious Nothing
Where the Rose ever
Blooms.

O, the Friend
Has done me a great favor
And has so thoroughly ruined my life,

What else would you expect
Seeing God would do!

Out of the ashes of this broken frame
There is a noble rising son pining for death,
Because,

Since we first met, Beloved,
I have become a foreigner
To every world
Except that one
In which there is only You
Or—Me.

Now that the heart has held
That which can never be touched
My subsistence is a blessed
Desolation

And from that I cry for more loneliness.

I am lonely.
I am so lonely, dear Beloved,
For the quintessence of
Loneliness,

For what is more alone than God?

Hafiz,
What is more pure and alone,

Magnificently Sovereign,
Than God.

NEEDING A MIRROR

Your
Eye
Is so wise

It keeps turning, turning
Needing to touch
Beauty.

It keeps turning,
Needing to find a mirror

That
Will caress you

As I.

ZIKR

Remembrance lowers the cup into
His luminous sky-well.

The mind often becomes plagued and can deny
The all-pervading beauty
Of God

When the great work of *zikr**
Is forgotten.

I have chained my every dancing atom
Into a divine seat in the Beloved's Tavern.

What I have learned
I am so eager to share:

Every ill will confess
It was just a lie

When the golden efforts of your love
Lift the precious wine
To your mouth.

Remembrance of our dear Friend
Lowers the soul's chalice
Into God.

Look, my sweet efforts and His Sublime Grace
Have now turned Creation into a single finger
On my hand

*Persian: remembrance

And from the vast reservoirs
In my heart and palms

Hafiz offers
God.

THE TENDER MOUTH

What will
The burial of my body be?

The pouring of a sacred cup of wine

Into the tender mouth of
The earth

And making
My dear sweet lover laugh

One more
Time.

GREETING GOD

I hear
The nightingale greeting
God.

I hear
The rain speaking to the roof
Of my heart.

Like a winter blanket of snow gently
Tucking in the earth

I let a great yearning within my ken
Lay down next
To Him.

I hear
A sorrowful lover being true
No matter what, even if the Beloved seems
Cruel.

Tonight
There is a jeweled falcon singing in a
Blessed pain using the tongue
Of

Hafiz.

REACHING TOWARD THE
MILLET FIELDS

It was beautiful,
It was so beautiful one night

We all began expecting to hear
God speak

In the waves reaching toward
The millet fields,

From the mouths of the hanging sky-ornaments
Crooning in light's intimate codes,

From the glances of plants and children
Playing with effulgent love.

Existence was so beautiful one night
We all began to expect
Our Beloved would
Speak

At the height of our wing's senses
That were stunned
Trying to comprehend the divine
Through the tiny organic
Filters,

That were stunned in glimpsing the reality
Of the thousand miraculous components
Of each moment
And step.

But we can't,
We can't yet hear God whistling inside,
So we weep.

We will all weep in some way
Until we
Do.

Lousy at Math

Once a group of thieves stole a rare diamond
Larger than a goose egg.

Its value could have easily bought
One thousand horses

And two thousand acres
Of the most fertile land in Shiraz.

The thieves got drunk that night
To celebrate their great haul,

But during the course of the evening
The effects of the liquor
And their mistrust of each other grew to such
An extent

They decided to divide the stone into pieces.
Of course then the Priceless became lost.

Most everyone is lousy at math
And does that to God—

Dissects the Indivisible One,

By thinking, saying,
"This is my Beloved, he looks like this
And acts like that,

How could that moron over there
Really
Be
God."

THE SUN IN DRAG

You are the Sun in drag.

You are God hiding from yourself.

Remove all the "mine"—that is the veil.

Why ever worry about

Anything?

Listen to what your friend Hafiz

Knows for certain:

The appearance of this world

Is a Magi's brilliant trick, though its affairs are

Nothing into nothing.

You are a divine elephant with amnesia

Trying to live in an ant

Hole.

Sweetheart, O sweetheart

You are God in

Drag!

BETWEEN OUR POLES

Who
Can I tell
The secrets of love?

Who has not confined their life
To a padded cell?

Look at
The nature of a river.
Its size, strength, and ability to give
Are often gauged by its width
And current.

God
Too moves between our poles, our depth.
He flows and gathers power between
Our heart's range of
Forgiveness and
Compassion.

Who
Can I tell,
Who can Hafiz tell tonight
All the secrets of
Love?

STAY CLOSE TO THOSE SOUNDS

The sun turns a key in a lock each day
As soon as it crawls out of bed.

Light swings open a door
And the many kinds of love rush out
Onto the infinite green field.

Your soul sometimes plays a note
Against the Sky's ear that excites
The birds and planets.

Stay close to any sounds
That make you glad you are alive.

Everything in this world is
Helplessly reeling.

An invisible wake was created
When God said to His beautiful dead lover,
"Be."

Hafiz, who will understand you
If you do not explain that last line?
Well then,

I will sing it this way,

When God said to Illusion,
"Be."

AN INVISIBLE PILE OF WOOD

It
Is often
Nothing the Master says

That keeps the desired fire in me
Alive.

Wherever the Master goes
An invisible pile of wood tags along

That he keeps throwing logs from
Onto my

Soul's hearth.

IT HAS NOT RAINED LIGHT

It has not rained light for many days.
The wells in most eyes look
Drought-stricken.

Thus friends are not easy to find
In this barren
Place

Where most everyone has become ill
From guarding
Nothing.

On this primal caravan
Careers and cities can appear real in this
Intense
Desert heat,

But I say to my close ones,

"Don't get lost in them,
It has not rained light there for days.

Look, most everyone is diseased
From 'making love' to
Nothing."

BERSERK

Once

In a while

God cuts loose His purse strings,

Gives a big wink to my orchestra.

Hafiz

Does not require

Any more prompting than that

To let

Every instrument inside

Go

Berserk.

NO MORE LEAVING

At
Some point
Your relationship
With God
Will
Become like this:

Next time you meet Him in the forest
Or on a crowded city street

There won't be anymore

"Leaving."

That is,

God will climb into
Your pocket.

You will simply just take

Yourself

Along!

WOW

Where does the real poetry
Come from?

From the amorous sighs
In this moist dark when making love
With form or
Spirit.

Where does poetry live?

In the eye that says, "Wow wee,"
In the overpowering felt splendor
Every sane mind knows
When it realizes—our life dance
Is only for a few magic
Seconds,

From the heart saying,
Shouting,

"I am so damn
Alive."

WHAT SHOULD WE DO
ABOUT THAT MOON?

A wine bottle fell from a wagon
And broke open in a field.

That night one hundred beetles and all their cousins
Gathered

And did some serious binge drinking.

They even found some seed husks nearby
And began to play them like drums and whirl.
This made God very happy.

Then the "night candle" rose into the sky
And one drunk creature, laying down his instrument,
Said to his friend—for no apparent
Reason,

"What should we do about that moon?"

Seems to Hafiz
Most everyone has laid aside the music

Tackling such profoundly useless
Questions.

Cupping My Hands Like a Mountain Valley

Like the way the valleys of the earth
Cup their hands for light and drink,

Like the way the desert opens up its sweet mouth
And laughs

When someone melts pearls in the sky
And rain, rain
Returns like a divine lover
With a hundred wonderful gifts

O, the words from the true Teacher
Bring my mind and cells
Such sacred nourishment and life.

When the moon is full
It gets gregarious and likes to chat.
I have heard it say,

"Look what can happen, dear seeker,
When you lean your graceful arms toward God in prayer,

Look at all that amorous light you can catch
That will help the night musicians and your soul
Get loose."

I stand revolving like a great dervish
In an ecstatic submission to His will.

I have been hired to perform the final act of grace.
I am the priest in every sacred wedding tent.

Tonight, I am a sovereign planet
With a great wool skirt.
I am a divine artist
On stage before God's entire court.

With each sublime whirl and orbit
I bow to the Sun's feet.
I fill my glass for you, dear pilgrim,
Beneath the luminous leaking barrel.

I then pour all the contents of my heart
And eye's experience
Upon this banquet table,

For your body and mind are a precious silk cloth
Hafiz has come to dye!

I circumambulate the Truth from the sky
Like a golden vulture.
I have forsaken all the crippling manners
Of even the most royal birds.

I carry a lute in my talons like a mortal weapon.
Please, please enter into a holy battle with me.
For I am God's friend
Who maims with compassion!
And you are a lost dove upon His wing.

I can teach you
How to bribe the Beloved with an angelic tune

So that the divine manna of His glance
Will fall upon your palate.

Some days I know
That you are en route to your own slaughter.

Some days I know
You are being trained as an emissary
To serve in His office of joy.

Dear one,
Last night, in the gallery of Reality
I saw a portrait I will never forget:

The Beloved was stirring a pot
With a spoon the size of a universe
And when He lifted it
I saw this whole world and its affairs
Were not even a floating speck of barley
Before the radiance of two diamonds
That were His brilliant cheeks!

All I could do when beholding that vision
Was to fall upon my knees

And cup my hands like a humble valley
Huddled between the thighs
Of this exquisite, holy mountain range

And try to build a reservoir to hold the Beloved's
Resplendent smile
That offers myriad tickets to freedom,
That offers the splendor of hearing God sing!

I am a spinning wheel upon the infinite.
I have swallowed that axis and hub
That fathered light and truth.

Grab hold and swing from me, my dear,
Doing the impossible
With your hands and feet both clapping.

I offer a mother's comfort and knowledge
To those who are tired and weak.

And when you become strong
I will conduct like a skilled warrior-king
Your divine volcanic glands exploding like new galaxies
In all their blessed madness.

God offers love, love, love
With His own hands,
To your beautiful parched holy mouth.

Open your soul, handsome dying one.
See all gender talk as a mighty joke,
In a oneness as glorious as this!

Hafiz, go running from that gallery
Like a naked, drunk lion
Roaring with a laughter that will shake
The whole earth
And every window and door throughout the sleeping
Cities,

Like a man,
Like a man who is delivering on a great steed
Fantastic news!

Tie yourself as a bell
To herds of mating camels
And spring flocks of clouds and birds.

Tie yourself to spawning stars
And to leaping whales
In a game of tag with the Moon!
Tie yourself to everything in creation
That got poured from God's magic hat.

O, tie your soul like a magnificent sweet chime
To every leaf and limb in existence,

Then begin to shout divine obscenities
So that He will surely send a tremendous storm.

Because Hafiz, because Hafiz,
O, sweet Hafiz,
You are a man with such benevolent and fantastic
Good News!

Dear wayfarer,
Now indulge me in a sober moment.
Please set down your glass.

I can help you write a letter of resignation
To all your fears and sadness.

Listen:
Let all movement and sound,
Let all movement and sound

Begin to speak the truth to your heart
And write its music upon your vision and
Soft pink tongue.

Soak all your prejudices in oil—
I would consider it a favor.
Bring and sing to me your darkest thoughts,
For my whole body is a blazing emerald wick,
I am a pure flame
Who needs and loves to burn your trash.

We should lean against each other more
In such a strange world as this
That can make you scared
And even believe in that lie called death.

We should support each other—
Give more warmth
In such a demanding world as this.

Let all movement
Gently yield something of God
Upon your chin and vision
And roll down onto your prayer mat
That will take root in the holy soil of your surrender.
May I hone your devotion with a kiss?

For all in existence is just spinning like this
Sweet earth
In a divine current.

Why not dance like Hafiz in the cup,
In the cup of His spoon?

I offer my clapping spirit to you,
That is in eternal movement.

Hafiz offers to bow at your feet
With hands that God has shaped and pounded.

Look into my palms, my dear,
They now contain your face and infinite existence.

All your ideas of space and time are shadows
That will run from this Sun He has made me.

I want to tie myself
As a gift around your neck.
I want to place a wonderful secret
Near your veins.

Why not use my verse as a golden camel bell
That you can turn upside down into a chalice
And fill with wine?

Hafiz,
You are a divine camel bell
That the Beloved is ringing with His own hand.

Hafiz, you were a blessed slave to Truth
That died like a cut reed and became hollow—

Turned into a divine instrument
That God now lifts to His own mouth,
Plays to summon this world to freedom.

How many men exist upon this earth
To whom I could whisper a holy secret?

Dear ones,
"God has sown Himself onto my tongue."

Like the way
The valleys of the earth
Cup their hands for light and drink,

Like
The way
The desert opens up its sweet mouth
And laughs

When someone melts pearls in the sky

And rain, rain
Returns like a divine lover
With a thousand wonderful
Gifts,

O, the luminous words of my Beloved
Now bring my mind and soul
Such a sacred
Nourishment
And

Peace.

WHY NOT BE POLITE

Everyone

Is God speaking.

Why not be polite and

Listen to

Him?

The God Who Only Knows Four Words

Every

Child

Has known God,

Not the God of names,

Not the God of don'ts,

Not the God who ever does

Anything weird,

But the God who only knows four words

And keeps repeating them, saying:

"Come dance with Me."

Come

Dance.

YOU WERE BRAVE
IN THAT HOLY WAR

You have done well
In the contest of madness.

You were brave in that holy war.

You have all the honorable wounds
Of one who has tried to find love

Where the Beautiful Bird
Does not drink.

May I speak to you
Like we are close
And locked away together?

Once I found a stray kitten
And I used to soak my fingers
In warm milk;

It came to think I was five mothers
On one hand.

Wayfarer,
Why not rest your tired body?
Lean back and close your eyes.

Come morning
I will kneel by your side and feed you.
I will so gently
Spread open your mouth

And let you taste something of my
Sacred mind and life.

Surely
There is something wrong
With your ideas of
God.

O, surely there is something wrong
With your ideas of
God

If you think
Our Beloved would not be so
Tender.

BRING THE MAN TO ME

A Perfect One was traveling through the desert.
He was stretched out around the fire one night
And said to one of his close ones,

"There is a slave loose not far from us.
He escaped today from a cruel master.
His hands are still bound behind his back,
His feet are also shackled.

I can see him right now praying for God's help.
Go to him.
Ride to that distant hill;
About a hundred feet up and to the right
You will find a small cave.
He is there.

Do not say a single word to him.
Bring the man to me.
God requests that I personally untie his body
And press my lips to his wounds."

The disciple mounts his horse and within two hours
Arrives at the small mountain cave.

The slave sees him coming, the slave looks frightened.
The disciple, on orders not to speak,
Gestures toward the sky, pantomiming:

God saw you in prayer,
Please come with me,

A great *Murshid** has used his heart's divine eye
To know your whereabouts.

The slave cannot believe this story,
And begins to shout at the man and tries to run

But trips from his bindings.
The disciple becomes forced to subdue him.

Think of this picture as they now travel:

The million candles in the sky are lit and singing.
Every particle of existence is a dancing alter
That some mysterious force worships.

The earth is a church floor whereupon
In the middle of a glorious night
Walks a slave, weeping, tied to a rope behind a horse,
With a speechless rider
Taking him toward the unknown.

Several times with all of his might the slave
Tries to break free,
Feeling he is being returned to captivity.
The rider stops, dismounts—brings his eyes
Near the prisoner's eyes.
A deep kindness there communicates an unbelievable hope.
The rider motions—soon, soon you will be free.
Tears roll down from the rider's cheeks
In happiness for this man.

Anger, all this fighting and tormenting want,

*Persian: teacher

*Mashuq,**
God has seen you and sent a close one.

Mashuq,
God has seen your heart in prayer
And sent Hafiz.

TOO BEAUTIFUL

The fire
Has roared near you.
The most intimate parts of your body
Got scorched,

So
Of course you have run
From your marriages into a
Different
House

That will shelter you
From embracing every aspect of Him.

God has
Roared near us.
The lashes on our heart's eye got burnt.
Of course we have
Run away

From His
Sweet flaming breath
That proposed an annihilation
Too real,

Too
Beautiful.

MY EYES SO SOFT

Don't
Surrender
Your loneliness so quickly.
Let it cut more
Deep.

Let it ferment and season you
As few human
Or even divine ingredients can.

Something missing in my heart tonight
Has made my eyes so soft,
My voice so
Tender,

My need of God
Absolutely
Clear.

THE DIAMOND TAKES SHAPE

Some parrots
Have become so skilled with
The human voice

They could give a brilliant discourse
About freedom and God

And an unsighted man nearby might
Even begin applauding with
The thought:

I just heard jewels fall from a
Great saint's mouth,

Though my Master used to say,

"The diamond takes shape slowly
With integrity's great force,

And from

The profound courage to never relinquish love."

Some parrots have become so skilled
With words,

The blind turn over their gold
And lives to caged

Feathers.

THAT DOES PERISH

The
Earth would die
If the sun stopped kissing her.

Hafiz is now such an exquisite world
That perishes

When God is not
Near.

CHAIN YOU TO MY BODY

All

These words

Are just a front.

What I would really like to do is

Chain you to my body,

Then sing for days

And days and

Days

About

God.

COVERS HER FACE
WITH BOTH HANDS

What
We speak
Becomes the house we live in.

Who will want to sleep in your bed
If the roof leaks
Right above
It?

Look what happens when the tongue
Cannot say to kindness,

"I will be your slave."

The moon
Covers her face with both hands

And can't bear
To look.

✳

DOG'S LOVE

All the crazy boys
Gather around their female
Counterpart,

When her canine beauty announces to the air
"My body is ready to play its part
In this miracle of
Birth."

Look what dedicated young men will do
For their chance moment
Of dancing ecstatic on their
Hind legs.

They will stay up all night
And howl.

They will forget about food for days and
Feverishly pray in their own language.

They will growl, make serious threats,
Even bite each other, saying,
"She's mine, all mine—watch out
You skinny fleabag."

Listen, human lovers:

When did you last keep a vigil
Beseeching
Light?

When did you last fast, lose twenty pounds,
In hopes of embracing
God?

Hafiz will give you the unedited news today:
You will need to outdo all the noble acts
Of
Dog's love.

TWENTY-TWO

Stay with Us

You
Leave
Our company when you speak
Of shame

And this makes
Everyone in the Tavern sad.

Stay with us
As we do the hardest work of rarely
Laying down
That pick and
Shovel

That will keep
Revealing our deeper kinship
With
God,

That will keep revealing
Our own divine
Worth.

You leave the company of the Beloved's friends
Whenever you speak of
Guilt,

And this makes
Everyone in the Tavern
Very sad.

Stay with us tonight
As we weave love

And reveal ourselves,
Reveal ourselves

As His precious
Garments.

I AM FULL OF LOVE TONIGHT

I am full of love tonight
Come look into my eyes, and let's go off
Sailing, my dear, on a long ocean ride.

This world will not touch you,
I will keep you snug upon my seat.

Let's plot
To make the moon jealous
With a radiance leaping from your cheek.

I will be full of love tonight,
Come look into these ancient eyes!

And let's go off sailing, my dear,
With our spirits intertwined.

Your body is just an old sandbar
In a speeding hourglass of time.

Love will turn the mouth of sorrow
Right side up.

Let your heart commence its destined
Laughing chime!

Hafiz will be brimful of love tonight,
Why ever be shy?

Come look into the playful eyes of my verse,
They are eternally branded,

Branded with
The Sun!

MANY LIVES AGO

Your tastes have become refined.

It used to be
If someone stole all your coins

Or locked your sexual pleasures in a room
You could not reach

This world would have no meaning
And a thirst for a hemlock brew
Might arise.

But that was many lives ago.

Now look at yourself:

You are often still a mess
Though these days,
At times,

You weep because
You miss
Him.

IT WILL STRETCH OUT
ITS LEG

All the classes you have sat in,
All the money you have paid
For "truth,"

Something must be wrong, though,
If your eye still wanders through the streets
Acting like a beggar.

Why not try this:
Let all the fake teachers starve.

Picture one of the great masters
In your mind,

Put your lips against his cheek
Each morning.

Say, keep saying,

"Dear Beloved, pinch me.
I want proof You're near—
A love-bruise on my rump will do."

The Friend is an unfathomable well
That knows everything;
Draw from that safe luminous sky.

Stay near this book,
It will stretch out its leg and
Trip you;

You'll fall
Into
God.

SOME OF THE PLANETS
ARE HOSTING

The ear becomes alert when music says,
"I am over here."

The eye goes on duty,
Becomes viable,

When beauty whistles and points to her dress
On the ground.

God has sent out ten thousand messengers
Announcing a great bash tonight some of the planets
Are hosting
Where the lead singer is God,
Himself.

But most of those couriers
Have become drunk, got waylaid,
Disoriented to the hilt
With such exalted
News,

And can no longer remember
The time and the
Place.

What does that have to do
With you?

Plenty.

Hafiz will fill you in later
If need
Be.

WHAT IS THE ROOT?

What

Is the

Root of all these

Words?

One thing: love.

But a love so deep and sweet

It needed to express itself

With scents, sounds, colors

That never before

Existed.

✺

THE SAME SUNTAN

Burn
Every address for
God.

Any
Beloved
Who has just one color of hair,
One gender, one race,

The same suntan all the time,
One rule book,

Trust me when I say,

That man is not even
Half a god

And will only
Cause you

Grief.

FOR THREE DAYS

Not many teachers in this world
Can give you as much enlightenment
In one year

As sitting all alone, for three days,
In your closet
Would
Do.

That means not leaving.
Better get a friend to help with
A few sandwiches
And
The chamber
Pot.

And no reading in there or writing poems,
That would be cheating;
Aim high—for a 360 degree
Detox.

This sitting alone, though, is
Not recommended

If you are normally
Sedated

Or have ever been under a doctor's
Surveillance because of your
Brain.

Dear one,
Don't let Hafiz fool you—

A ruby is buried
Here.

A Clever Piece of Mutton

Like a
Clever piece of mutton
Refusing to go down the "well"

Knowing it will so quickly just come out
The "other end"

So it lodges itself between one's teeth—

That's the kind of poem Hafiz
Wants to sing
Today.

WHO CAN HEAR
THE BUDDHA SING?

Hafiz,
Tonight as you sit with your
Young students

Who
Have eyes
Burning like coals for the truth,

Raise your glass in honor
Of The Old Great One from Asia,

Speak in the beautiful style
And precision wit of a
Japanese verse.

Say a profound truth about this path
With the edge of your sailor's tongue that
Has been honed on the finest sake.

Okay, dear ones, are you ready?
Are you braced?

Well then:

Who can hear the Buddha sing
If that dog between your legs is barking?

Who can hear the Buddha sing
If that canine between your
Thighs

Still
Wants to do circus

Tricks?

BUTTERING THE SKY

Slipping

On my shoes,

Boiling water,

Toasting bread,

Buttering the sky:

That should be enough contact

With God in one day

To make anyone

Crazy.

HOW FASCINATING

How

Fascinating the idea of death

Can be.

Too bad, though,

Because

It just isn't

True.

WHERE GREAT LIONS
LOVE TO PISS

A royal temple has been built
In a sacred forest

On the exact spot
Where for thousands of years
Great lions have loved to piss.

God does not like this:

His cherished beasts
No longer able to leave
Their holy scent in the jungle
Near a favorite resting spot of God's
Left toe.

My dear,
I am about as far
From a sacrilegious man as this
World can endure,

For I
Have found the power
To say "no" to any actions
That might harm myself
Or another.

Listen:

Love reveals man is so endowed
To "lift his leg"
Upon galaxies.

A POTENT LOVER

The sun and the moon shiver

When I drop my pants.

Beware

Of this potent

Lover.

❋

AN ASTRONOMICAL QUESTION

What
Would
Happen if God leaned down

And gave you a full wet
Kiss?

Hafiz
Doesn't mind answering astronomical questions
Like that:

You would surely start
Reciting all day, inebriated,

Rogue-poems
Like
This.

I WISH I COULD SPEAK
LIKE MUSIC

I wish I could speak like music.

I wish I could put the swaying splendor
Of the fields into words

So that you could hold Truth
Against your body
And dance.

I am trying the best I can
With this crude brush, the tongue,

To cover you with light.

I wish I could speak like divine music.

I want to give you the sublime rhythms
Of this earth and the sky's limbs

As they joyously spin and surrender,
Surrender
Against God's luminous breath.

Hafiz wants you to hold me
Against your precious
Body

And dance,
Dance.

IN A CIRCUS BOOTH

Why let
A fortune-teller in a circus booth
Advise your heart?

Out of ten thousand people who say
They can read the fine print on a star

One might have that great gift,
That remarkable vision to
Know the future.

Better to let one like Hafiz become your guide
To our needed sobriety on this path.

Be a friend to your heirs and purse,
Listen:

Most astrologers, psychics, and "healers"
Would do more good for this world—

Flipping soy burgers
Somewhere.

Why seek guidance about your life
And God

From a grinning coiled snake
In a carnival
Show?

MAYBE EVEN LUCRATIVE

A
New fish in town
Said to an old fish,

"Where can a young pretty girl like me
Meet some handsome, strong fins?

And the old fish replied,

"I said those same words
When I first found myself in this
Corner of the ocean."

I am sure
I could concoct
A charming ending to this
Poem

That might even seem profound,
Maybe even life-changing,
Maybe even lucrative?

If that happens—

I'll write.

TROUBLED

Troubled?
Then stay with me, for I'm not.

Lonely?
A thousand naked amorous ones dwell in ancient caves
Beneath my eyelids.

Riches?
Here's a pick,
My whole body is an emerald that begs,
"Take me."

Write all that worries you on a piece of parchment;
Offer it to God.
Even from the distance of a millennium

I can lean the flame in my heart
Into your life

And turn
All that frightens you
Into holy
Incense
Ash.

The Silk Mandala

The
Spider and the lizard
Grabbed hold of each other's mouth
Because of
Love.

The details
Of their affections
Most would not like to
Hear,

Though I watched for a while,
As God might,
Their holy dance

Spinning
From one thread that hung
From the silk
Mandala.

I watched until they fell,
As our own bodies someday will,

Panting
Like a great falling
Star.

A FOREST HERB

Some poets have the skill to talk
About God

Without ever using any of His pseudonyms.

Some have such skill
You do not need to walk to the river
With your bucket.

They, with words' magnetism,
Can coax Venus from her primal orbit and steal
From her mouth
That one drop of miraculous dew
She has been collecting in her veins
Since time said,
"I Am."

I will wear
All the common garb of the tongue
If it will win me your friendship.

I will turn myself into a
Forest
Herb

If
You will
Apply me to your
Wounds.

YOUR CAMEL IS
LOADED TO SING

The

Camel

Is loaded to sing.

Look what good poetry can do:

Untie the knot in the burlap sack

And lift the golden

Falcon

Out.

STEALING BACK THE FLUTE

Something
In your soul trusts
Me

Otherwise it would not let you near
These words.

God has spilled a Great One
Into each of us,

This warrior is always fearless
But also always
Kind.

The only business I am concerned
With these
Days,

Since I heard the Moon's drunk
Singing,

Is
Stealing
Back our flute from
Krishna.

WHERE THE DRUM
LOST ITS MIND

You are one of us now
Because you cannot forget His beauty.

If we all lifted our shirts in unison
The stitch marks around our blessed wounds
Could all join hands and commiserate
For hours.

Near the campsite of love
The drum
Lost its mind,

Thus our eyes now wear God's
Royal seal.

Look,
Huma's* wing
Cast a great shadow upon this earth
And there the world wisely built a thousand temples
Whose pillar-arms reach up toward Him.

I see you have the luminous afflictions
From visiting His oasis of light,
From visiting God's own private chamber.
Indeed, indeed,
You are one of us.

And the golden drum

*Persian: the mythological Bird of Paradise that never touches ground

That surrenders its life
Will come to so sweetly play,

So divinely laugh,
Like Hafiz.

EVERY CITY IS A DULCIMER

There is
The rising up
From light's embrace
You can see in a summer field or
In a child's dancing.

Every city is a dulcimer
That plays its chorus against
Our ears.

The lid of a pot starts jumping
When water gets ecstatic from fire.

If I ever don't complete a sentence
While we are together
Accept my apologies and try to understand
This sweet drunk thought.

Birds initially had no desire to fly,
What really happened was this:

God once sat close to them playing
Music.

When He left
They missed Him so much
Their great longing sprouted wings,
Needing to search the
Sky.

Listen,
Hafiz knows,

Nothing evolves us like
Love.

RUIN

Sometimes love tastes like this:

The pain so sweet
I beg God,

"May I never open my eyes again
And know another image
Than what I have
Just seen.

May I never know
Another feeling other than your
Inconceivable
Immaculate
Touch.

Why not
Let Hafiz die
In this blessed
Ruin."

BETWEEN YOUR EYE
AND THIS PAGE

Between
Your eye and this page
I am standing.

Between
Your ear and sound
The Friend has pitched a golden tent
Your spirit walks through a thousand times
A day.

Each time you pass the Kaaba
The Sun unwinds a silk thread from your body.
Each time you pass any object
From within it
I bow.

If you are still having doubts
About His nearness

Once in a while debate with God.

Between
Your eye and this page Hafiz
Is standing.

Bump
Into me
More.

PRACTICE THIS NEW BIRDCALL

The way we live opens windows
And calls in a secret voice to anything
Still missing.

There is nothing in your mind
You have not invited in.

There is no event in your life
You in some way
Did not drive a hard bargain for.

We were all once like moons,
Often full and bright.

The heart, in its wisdom,
Ceaselessly shops for
Him.

The wise in any foreign country
Seek a true guide.

The guide says,

"Just practice this new birdcall,
It will attract to you
Something even
Greater than

Love."

TWENTY-FIVE

I Know I Was the Water

Who can believe the divine kindness of God?
Who can comprehend what happens when
Separation ends?

For now,
Because of my union with Reality,
Now,
Whenever I hear a story of one of His prophets
Having come into this world,

I know I was a tree that stood near,
Leaned down and took notes.

I know I was the earth that measured the infinite
Arch in His feet.

I know I was the water,
I know I was the food and water that nourished Him—
That went into our Beloved's mouth.

Pilgrim,
If it is your wish, you will someday see
You sat inside of Hafiz

And it was with the lyre you gave me
We sang of truth and the sublime intimacy:

"I know I was the water
That quenched the Christ's thirst.

I know I Am the food and water that goes
Into every
Mouth."

WITH THAT MOON LANGUAGE

Admit something:

Everyone you see, you say to them,
"Love me."

Of course you do not do this out loud;
Otherwise,
Someone would call the cops.

Still though, think about this,
This great pull in us
To connect.

Why not become the one
Who lives with a full moon in each eye
That is always saying,

With that sweet moon
Language,

What every other eye in this world
Is dying to
Hear.

WITHOUT BRUSHING MY HAIR

The
Closer
I get to you, Beloved,
The more I can see
It is just You and I all alone
In this
World.

I hear
A knock at my door,
Who else could it be,
So I rush without brushing
My hair.

For too
Many nights
I have begged for Your
Return

And what
Is the use of vanity
At this late hour, at this divine season,
That has now come to my folded
Knees?

If your love letters are true dear God
I will surrender myself to
Who You keep saying
I
Am.

INTEGRITY

Few
Have the strength
To be a real
Hero—

That rare
Man or woman
Who always keeps
Their
Word.

Even an angel needs rest.
Integrity creates a body so vast

A thousand winged ones will
Plead,

"May I lay my cheek
Against
You?"

THERE

There
I bow my head—
At the feet of every creature.

This constant submission and homage,
Of kissing God
All over,

Someday,
Every lover will
Do.

Only
There I prostrate myself—
Against the beauty of each form—

For when I bring
My heart close to any object
I always hear the Friend
Say,

"Hafiz, I am
Here."

WHEN SPACE IS NOT RATIONED

For a while
The eagle in flight might say,

"Look dear, I am home—
Space is no longer being rationed."

For a while you might feel
I am complete,

When the touch from another upon certain
Of your fields

Has the power to dissolve all that
Is known.

Wholeness, I think,
Draws its life somewhere where the breathing
Stops,

Somewhere where the mind cradles light,
Where the only senses that remain

Blush and stumble
If they try to speak with our language so new
It is still trying to
Invent,

Still shaping
Its first intelligible sound,
Still sculpting its first true image of
God.

BIRDS OF PASSAGE

The
Classroom
Surely becomes disarrayed
When the teacher is out of sight
Because of our grand
Volcanic
Spirits.

The
Birds of passage
Arrive with a broken
Wing,

Though
Are then lifted by God
So high and
"Low"

To experience the heart
Of everything.

The mind surely becomes disarrayed
When the Teacher is out
Of sight.

ACT GREAT

What is the key
To untie the knot of your mind's suffering?

What
Is the esoteric secret
To slay the crazed one whom each of us
Did wed

And who can ruin
Our heart's and eye's exquisite tender
Landscape?

Hafiz has found
Two emerald words that
Restored
Me

That I now cling to as I would sacred
Tresses of my Beloved's
Hair:

Act great.
My dear, always act great.

What is the key
To untie the knot of the mind's suffering?

Benevolent thought, sound
And movement.

THE ONLY MATERIAL

What

A

Skilled man can do with a

Hammer

The advanced pilgrim can do with

Thought.

One builds their own seat in this world

Using God—

The only material,

That is

E
v
e
r
y
w
h
e
r
e
.

I GOT KIN

Plant
So that your own heart
Will grow.

Love
So God will think,

"Ahhhhh,
I got kin in that body!
I should start inviting that soul over
For coffee and
Rolls."

Sing
Because this is a food
Our starving world
Needs.

Laugh
Because that is the purest
Sound.

ONLY ONE RULE

The sky
Is a suspended blue ocean.
The stars are the fish that swim.

The planets are the white whales I sometimes
Hitch a ride
On,

The sun and all light
Have forever fused themselves into my heart
And upon my
Skin.

There is only one rule on this Wild Playground,

Every sign Hafiz has ever seen
Reads the same.

They all say,

"Have fun, my dear; my dear, have fun,
In the Beloved's divine
Game,

O, in the Beloved's
Wonderful
Game."

YOUR THOUSAND LIMBS

Your thousand limbs rend my body.

This is the way to die:

Beauty keeps laying

Its sharp knife

Against

Me.

AND LOVE SAYS

And love
Says,

"I will, I will take care of you,"

To everything that is
Near.